STEP-BY-STEP
DELICIOUS

LEARN TO COOK
YOUR FAVORITE DISHES
IN 7 STEPS OR LESS

Recipes by Catrine Kelty | Photography by Adam DeTour

Brimming with creative inspiration, how-to projects, and useful information to enrich your everyday life, Quarto Knows is a favorite destination for those pursuing their interests and passions. Visit our site and dig deeper with our books into your area of interest: Quarto Creates, Quarto Cooks, Quarto Homes, Quarto Lives, Quarto Drives, Quarto Explores, Quarto Gifts, or Quarto Kids.

The Harvard Common Press titles are also available at discount for retail, wholesale, promotional, and bulk purchase. For details, contact the Special Sales Manager by email at specialsales@quarto.com or by mail at The Quarto Group, Attn: Special Sales Manager, 401 Second Avenue North, Suite 310, Minneapolis, MN 55401, USA.

22 21 20 19 18   1 2 3 4 5

ISBN: 978-1-55832-944-7

Digital edition published in 2018

Library of Congress Cataloging-in-Publication Data available

Design by Amanda Richmond
Photograph and Food Styling: Adam DeTour

Printed in China

C41.5

Catrine Kelty is a Boston-based food stylist who has been named a food stylist "Instagrammer to Watch" by VSCO, and Shelby Publishing included her in its list of "Women of Influence in the Food Industry," in 2017. Her recipes have been published in *The Coastal Table* magazine and *Feast for the Eyes.* She has styled for many magazines and numerous cookbooks. You can learn more about Catrine by visiting www.ckfoodstylist.com.

Adam DeTour is a commercial and editorial photographer who specializes in portraits and food. His photography has appeared in *Edible Boston, Boston* magazine, *Inc* magazine, and the *New York Times,* among other online and print venues. He has lived in New Hampshire, New York, and Italy and now lives and works in Boston.

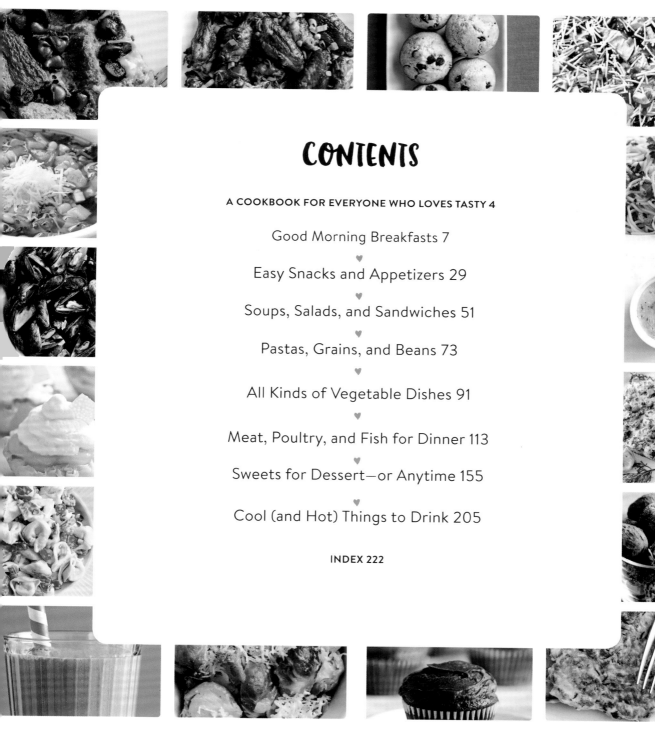

CONTENTS

WE REALLY LOVE RECIPE VIDEOS . . .

. . . and we are guessing you do, too, if you picked up this book. A couple of years ago, we discovered the amazing food videos that were taking over social media and the Internet, from brands like Tasty, Well Done, Delish, and Food Network.

They changed the way we cook. The fast-paced, not-too-long videos that show exactly what you need to buy, what cooking steps you need to perform, and best of all, a yummy picture of what you get to eat when you're done, all made cooking seem easier, quicker, and more exciting than we thought possible. Kids we know who didn't think they could cook now realize they can. Grownups we know, even ones who are expert cooks, prop up their phones or tablets on the kitchen counter and cook in a new and fun way.

. . . AND WE REALLY LOVE COOKBOOKS . . .

.. . . for many reasons. We like to give cookbooks as gifts. Many of our favorite recipes are ones we found in cookbooks. In a food video, you have to scroll backward and forward to find the step you need, but in a cookbook, it's all conveniently there on a page. We like to write in the margins of our cookbooks—things like "I doubled the sugar" or "I used an orange instead of a lemon" remind us of how we changed a recipe to make it our very own. And those chocolate stains on page 54? They remind us of the gooey, messy brownies we made with our friends one weekend, and that makes us smile and laugh.

… and so we decided to combine our two loves in this book.

One day, we noticed a friend who had taped screenshots from a food video to the kitchen counter. They looked kind of like pages from a book. Hmmm . . . that made us think. Could we create a cookbook, with lots and lots of step-by-step photos, that would capture the vibe and spirit of online food videos? We set out to do so, and here is the result. It's our way to pay homage to this new way of cooking and to do so in a medium—cookbooks—that has given us loads of good times in the kitchen. It's our gift to our fellow fans. We hope you like it.

Love and dishes,
XOXO

GOOD MORNING
BREAKFASTS

JAM-FILLED CRÊPES

Crêpes are really very easy to make, yet they are so impressive to serve. Be sure to use a 7- or 8-inch (18 or 20 cm) skillet or else your crêpes will end up too thin and they will tear when you try to fill them. Also, treat them gently when flipping them—they are more delicate than pancakes. You might tear one or two until you get the hang of it, but they'll still be scrumptious.

HERE'S WHAT YOU NEED

1 cup (125 g) all-purpose flour
1⅓ cups (315 ml) milk
3 large eggs
1 tablespoon (13 g) sugar
¼ teaspoon salt
3 tablespoons (42 g) unsalted butter, melted, plus more for the pan
Your favorite jam, for serving

HERE'S WHAT YOU GET

6 TO 8 BRUNCH-WORTHY CRÊPES

HERE'S WHAT YOU DO

1. Combine the flour, milk, eggs, sugar, salt, and the 3 tablespoons (45 ml) of melted butter in a blender and blend for a minute or two until thoroughly combined and bubbly.

A TASTY TIP Think of crêpes like a blank canvas: For a heartier breakfast crêpe, layer in thinly sliced fruit of your choice. Or turn these into dessert crêpes by spreading on Nutella or caramel sauce instead of jam!

2. Transfer the batter to a bowl and let rest at room temperature for 30 minutes.

4. Pour 3 to 4 tablespoons (45 to 55 g) of the batter into the pan and swirl to cover the bottom of the whole pan with the batter. Cook for 2 to 3 minutes until the edges of the crêpe brown and recede.

3. Heat a 7- or 8-inch (18 or 20 cm) nonstick skillet over medium-high heat and brush lightly with melted butter.

5. With a thin spatula, lift the crêpe and flip over to cook for another minute or so until it's golden.

6. Transfer the crêpe to a plate, spread it with a thin layer of jam, roll it up, and serve.

FRESH BLUEBERRY PANCAKES

Whether you call them flapjacks, griddlecakes, hotcakes, or pancakes, the sizzle of hot batter in the pan will make you glad you dragged yourself out of bed. Blueberries are a classic and delicious sweet-tart addition.

HERE'S WHAT YOU NEED

1 cup (125 g) all-purpose flour
1 teaspoon baking powder
¼ teaspoon ground cinnamon
3 tablespoons (42 g) unsalted butter, melted
3 tablespoons (45 g) light brown sugar
¾ cup (175 ml) milk
1 large egg, separated
¾ cup (190 g) fresh blueberries
4 tablespoons (55 g) unsalted butter, melted, mixed with ¼ cup (60 ml) vegetable oil
Maple syrup, for serving

HERE'S WHAT YOU GET

8 FLUFFY PANCAKES

HERE'S WHAT YOU DO

1. In a bowl, whisk together the flour, baking powder, and cinnamon.

Variations

For banana pancakes, substitute 1 overripe mashed banana (1 cup [225 g]) for the blueberries and add ¼ teaspoon ground ginger to the dry ingredients.

For chocolate chip pancakes, substitute ⅓ cup (58 g) of chocolate chips for the blueberries.

2. In a larger bowl, mix the 3 tablespoons (45 ml) melted butter, sugar, milk, and the egg yolk. Mix well to combine.

3. In a third bowl, whisk the egg white until stiff.

5. Heat a griddle or skillet over medium-high heat. It is ready when a drop of water beads up on its surface. When ready, drop a tablespoon (15 ml) of the butter-oil mixture into the pan.

6. Without crowding the pan, pour in scoops of about ¼ cup (55 g) batter for each pancake. Cook on medium-high heat until they start to bubble and then turn over and cook for another minute or two until golden.

7. Serve the pancakes immediately, as you make them, with butter and maple syrup.

4. Stir the dry ingredients into the wet ingredients, mixing well to combine them. Fold in the egg white and then the blueberries. Let the batter sit at room temperature for 20 to 30 minutes.

FRUITS with TRIPLE GINGER SAUCE

This creamy sauce packs a gingery wallop. The yogurt keeps it healthy, and the bit of sour cream adds tangy richness. Experiment with different fruit combinations: bananas and pineapple; or apples, pears, and grapes; or mixed berries and melon.

HERE'S WHAT YOU NEED

2½ cups (575 g) whole-milk vanilla Greek-style yogurt

½ cup (115 g) sour cream

⅓ cup (75 g) packed dark brown sugar

½ cup (48 g) finely chopped crystallized ginger

2 tablespoons (12 g) minced or (16 g) grated fresh ginger

1½ tablespoons (8 g) ground ginger

Your favorite fruits, cut into bite-size pieces, for serving

HERE'S WHAT YOU GET

8 TO 10 SPICY-SWEET SERVINGS OF SAUCE

A TASTY TIP If you want a slightly less spicy ginger sauce, cut back a little on either the fresh ginger or the ground ginger. Don't skimp on the crystallized ginger, though.

HERE'S WHAT YOU DO

1. In a medium bowl, whisk together the yogurt and sour cream to blend.

3. Scrape the sides of the bowl with a flexible spatula and add the yogurt–sour cream mixture.

2. In a food processor, process the brown sugar, crystallized ginger, fresh ginger, and ground ginger until they are well combined, about 40 seconds.

4. Process to blend well, about 30 seconds, stopping to scrape the sides of the bowl as needed.

5. Transfer to a bowl, cover, and refrigerate until you're ready to use the sauce. Serve with your favorite fruits.

RICH FRENCH TOAST

You can make French toast with practically any bread, but thick slices of a fluffy, eggy bread with a bit of sugar in it, like brioche or challah, will soak up the egg-milk dip beautifully and develop a delicately crispy crust in the skillet, making for a luxurious morning treat.

HERE'S WHAT YOU NEED

4 large eggs

1 cup (235 ml) milk

½ cup (120 ml) heavy cream

1 tablespoon (15 ml) vanilla extract

1 teaspoon ground cinnamon

¼ teaspoon salt

4 tablespoons (55 g) unsalted butter, melted, mixed with ¼ cup (60 ml) vegetable oil

6 thick slices of egg-based bread, such as brioche or challah (day-old is best)

Maple syrup, confectioners' sugar, and/or fresh berries, for serving

HERE'S WHAT YOU GET

4 TO 6 DECADENT SERVINGS

A TASTY TIP Serve this with the Mixed Berry Coulis on page 178.

HERE'S WHAT YOU DO

1. In a large shallow bowl, whisk together the eggs, milk, and cream.

3. Heat 2 tablespoons (28 ml) of the butter-oil mixture in a 12-inch (30 cm) nonstick skillet over medium-high heat. Dip the bread slices into the egg mixture on both sides, making sure the slices are completely covered with the mixture.

2. Add the vanilla, cinnamon, and salt to the liquid ingredients and stir to combine.

4. Transfer the bread slices to the skillet and cook for 2 to 3 minutes per side until golden.

5. Serve the French toast right away, with maple syrup, confectioners' sugar, and/or berries.

CREAMY SCRAMBLED EGGS ON ENGLISH MUFFINS

Both milk and sour cream enrich these eggs. If you have time to sit down for a few minutes on a weekday morning, serve these breakfast sandwiches open-face, with a knife and fork. But if you've hit the snooze button one too many times, close up the English muffins and eat 'em on the go!

HERE'S WHAT YOU NEED

4 large eggs
2 tablespoons (28 ml) milk
½ teaspoon salt
¼ teaspoon ground black pepper
2 tablespoons (28 g) unsalted butter
2 tablespoons (30 g) sour cream
2 English muffins, split, toasted, and buttered
2 scallions, thinly sliced

HERE'S WHAT YOU GET

2 WEEKDAY-BREAKFAST SERVINGS

HERE'S WHAT YOU DO

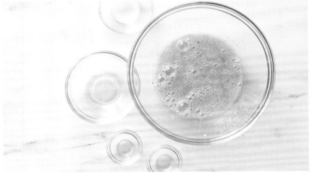

1. Beat the eggs, milk, salt, and pepper together in a small bowl.

A TASTY TIP This is a quick and satisfying breakfast. If you have another minute or two in the morning, add Canadian bacon to the sandwiches. Or sprinkle some shredded Cheddar or mozzarella cheese onto the bottoms of the toasted English muffins. When you put the hot scrambled eggs on top, the cheese will melt.

2. Melt the butter in a 10-inch (25 cm) nonstick skillet over medium heat.

4. As the eggs start to set, quickly add the sour cream and continue cooking until the eggs are thick and no longer wet.

3. Pour the egg mixture into the skillet and, using a spatula, carefully move the eggs back and forth, creating large soft curds.

5. Divide the eggs on top of the English muffins and sprinkle with the scallions.

6. Serve the sandwiches hot, either closed up or open-faced.

CINNAMON— CHOCOLATE CHIP MUFFINS

Chocolate and cinnamon has long been a classic flavor combination in Mexico, and it's becoming more and more popular everywhere—with good reason. Here, the cinnamon adds a spicy note to the sweet, rich, chocolate-studded muffins.

HERE'S WHAT YOU NEED

Nonstick cooking spray (optional)
2 cups (250 g) all-purpose flour
⅔ cup (133 g) sugar
2½ teaspoons (12 g) baking powder
¼ teaspoon baking soda
1 teaspoon ground cinnamon
½ teaspoon salt
1 cup (235 ml) milk
2 large eggs
½ cup (1 stick, or 110 g) unsalted butter, melted
1 cup (175 g) semisweet chocolate chips

HERE'S WHAT YOU GET

12 TO 16 DECADENT MUFFINS

Variation

For blueberry muffins, simply switch out the chocolate chips for 1 cup (145 g) of small blueberries.

HERE'S WHAT YOU DO

1. Preheat the oven to 400°F (200°C, or gas mark 6). Grease 12 to 16 muffin cups with nonstick cooking spray or line with paper liners. In a large bowl, mix the flour, sugar, baking powder, baking soda, cinnamon, and salt.

3. Add the wet ingredients to the dry ingredients and mix with a spatula or wooden spoon until evenly wet, but be careful not to overmix. Fold in the chocolate chips.

2. In another bowl, whisk together the milk and eggs until thoroughly combined and then whisk in the melted butter.

4. Spoon the batter into the prepared muffin pans, filling each muffin cup three-quarters full.

5. Bake for 15 to 20 minutes until a toothpick inserted in the middle of a muffin comes out clean. Let cool for 8 to 10 minutes before serving.

CHEDDAR BACON MUFFINS

These cheesy muffins, with their hit of salty bacon and chopped scallions, are a great antidote for when you are tired of sweet breakfast muffins. They'd also be great served alongside a soup or a salad at lunchtime or dinnertime.

HERE'S WHAT YOU NEED

Nonstick cooking spray (optional)
2 cups (250 g) all-purpose flour
2 tablespoons (26 g) sugar
2 teaspoons baking powder
½ teaspoon baking soda
½ teaspoon salt
1 cup (235 ml) milk
⅓ cup (80 ml) corn oil
1 large egg
6 slices of bacon, cooked and crumbled
3 scallions, thinly sliced
1 cup (115 g) shredded Cheddar cheese, divided

HERE'S WHAT YOU GET

12 SAVORY MUFFINS

HERE'S WHAT YOU DO

1. Preheat the oven to 400°F (200°C, or gas mark 6). Grease a 12-cup muffin pan with nonstick cooking spray or line with paper liners. In a large bowl, whisk together the flour, sugar, baking powder, baking soda, and salt.

A TASTY TIP Split these savory muffins in half and use them as the bread for your morning fried-egg sandwich.

2. In another bowl, whisk together the milk, corn oil, and egg.

4. Fold in the bacon, scallions, and ¾ cup (90 g) of the Cheddar cheese, making sure all the ingredients are evenly distributed.

3. Using a spatula, stir the wet ingredients into the dry ingredients, mixing well to combine them.

5. Fill the muffin cups three-quarters full with the batter and sprinkle the tops with the remaining ¼ cup (25 g) of cheese.

6. Bake for 20 minutes or until the muffin tops are golden and a toothpick inserted in the middle of the muffins comes out dry. Cool for 5 minutes before serving.

SMOKED SALMON BREAKFAST SANDWICHES

Classic New York deli flavors couldn't be easier to re-create at home. Set out a brunch bar of the ingredients and let everyone assemble their own sandwich. Spreading a little bit of the cream cheese on both the top and bottom halves of the bagel helps keep the tomato and cucumber slices from sliding around.

HERE'S WHAT YOU NEED

4 ounces (115 g) cream cheese, softened
1 tablespoon (10 g) minced red onion
1 tablespoon (4 g) chopped fresh dill
1 tablespoon (9 g) capers, rinsed and drained
1 teaspoon grated lemon zest
4 bagels (flavor of your choice), cut in half and toasted
4 ounces (115 g) sliced smoked salmon
1 large tomato, thinly sliced
16 thin slices of English cucumber
1 cup (20 g) baby arugula

HERE'S WHAT YOU GET

4 BAGEL SANDWICHES

A TASTY TIP You can use any kind of cured salmon in this sandwich: hot-smoked, cold-smoked, or gravlax. Try them all to see what you like best.

HERE'S WHAT YOU DO

1. In a small bowl, mix the cream cheese, onion, dill, capers, and lemon zest into a smooth spread.

2. Divide the cream cheese mixture among the bagels, spreading some on the top and bottom of each bagel half.

3. Top each bottom bagel half with 1 ounce (28 g) of the smoked salmon.

4. Top the salmon with 2 tomato slices, 4 cucumber slices, and ¼ cup (5 g) of the arugula.

5. Top each loaded-up bottom bagel half with the top bagel. Cut in half and serve.

BACON, CHEESE, and ONION QUICHE

A quiche is basically a baked egg tart. Unlike frittatas, quiches always have crusts. And the eggs are usually mixed with cream and cheese to make a more custardy sort of filling. This is my version of a classic quiche Lorraine, which traditionally includes bacon, Swiss (or Gruyére) cheese, and onions.

HERE'S WHAT YOU NEED

1 pie shell (½ of a package of refrigerated pie dough)
2 cups (390 g) uncooked rice or (430 g) dried beans (for pie weights)
2 tablespoons (28 ml) olive oil
1 large yellow onion, thinly sliced
½ teaspoon salt
½ teaspoon ground black pepper
6 slices of bacon, cooked and crumbled
3 large eggs
1 cup (235 ml) half-and-half
1 cup (110 g) shredded Swiss or (115 g) Cheddar cheese, divided

HERE'S WHAT YOU GET

6 TO 8 EGGY SERVINGS

HERE'S WHAT YOU DO

1. Preheat the oven to 350°F (230°C, or gas mark 8). Line a 9-inch (23 cm) quiche or tart pan (with or without a removable bottom) that is at least 1¼ inches (3 cm) deep with the pie dough, making sure it goes all the way up the sides. Line the dough with a piece of parchment paper and add 2 cups (390 g) of uncooked rice or (430 g) dried beans (for pie weights) to cover the bottom of the pan all the way to the edges. Refrigerate for 15 minutes.

2. Bake the crust for 10 to 15 minutes. Carefully lift the parchment without dropping any of the pie weights, prick the dough with a fork, and bake for another 2 minutes or until the dough lightly browns. Set aside to cool. Once cool, you can save the rice or the beans in a container to use as pie weights for your next quiche.

4. Transfer the onions and bacon into the quiche crust.

5. In a bowl, whisk together the eggs, half-and-half, and ½ cup (55 to 58 g) of the cheese. Pour on top of the bacon and eggs in the crust. Sprinkle evenly with the remaining ½ cup (55 to 58 g) of cheese.

6. Bake for 30 to 35 minutes until the quiche is puffed and golden. Serve warm or at room temperature.

3. Turn the oven down to 375°F (190°C, or gas mark 5). Heat the olive oil in a large skillet over medium heat and cook the onions until soft and golden about 10 minutes. Season with the salt and pepper.

EGG AND CHEESE BREAKFAST BURRITOS

If you've got a big breakfast appetite, spread each tortilla with a couple of tablespoons (32 g) of warm refried beans before adding the eggs and toppings. This adds even more nutrition and fiber, too.

HERE'S WHAT YOU NEED

4 large eggs
1 tablespoon (15 ml) milk
1 teaspoon dried oregano
½ teaspoon ground cumin
½ teaspoon salt
¼ teaspoon ground black pepper
2 tablespoons (28 g) unsalted butter
½ cup (58 g) shredded Cheddar cheese,
   plus more as desired
4 burrito-size flour tortillas, warmed
Salsa, diced avocado, and/or chopped
   red onion or thinly sliced scallions (optional)

HERE'S WHAT YOU GET

4 WARM BURRITOS

HERE'S WHAT YOU DO

1. In a bowl, whisk the eggs, milk, oregano, cumin, salt, and pepper.

2. In a 10-inch (25 cm) nonstick skillet, melt the butter over medium heat. Cook the eggs in the butter, gently stirring and making large soft curds with a spatula.

3. Add the Cheddar cheese and let it melt into the eggs. Cook, stirring gently, until the mixture is no longer wet.

4. Divide the egg-cheese mixture into the middle of each tortilla, forming it into a line. Top the eggs with salsa, avocado, onions, or scallions, and more cheese, if desired.

5. Fold the burritos by bringing the top and bottom of each tortilla together and then folding the sides into the middle, like an envelope. Serve right away.

EASY SNACKS and APPETIZERS

CLASSIC DEVILED EGGS

Deviled eggs make great party food, and this recipe is easily doubled or even tripled. The egg yolk filling can take on many flavors; check out the variations below for a few ideas. Whatever variations you choose, it's always nice to garnish your deviled eggs with a bit of something that hints at the flavor of the filling.

HERE'S WHAT YOU NEED

6 large eggs
¼ cup (60 g) mayonnaise
1 teaspoon Dijon mustard
Salt and ground black pepper to taste
Paprika, for garnish

HERE'S WHAT YOU GET

12 STUFFED EGG HALVES

Variations

Add 1 teaspoon curry powder to the filling mixture and top each egg with a golden raisin.

Add 1 cooked and crumbled slice of bacon to the filling mixture and top each egg with a sprinkle of chopped scallions.

Substitute plain Greek-style yogurt for the mayonnaise and top each egg with a bit of finely chopped cucumber or a sliver of Kalamata olive.

HERE'S WHAT YOU DO

1. Put the eggs in a single layer in the bottom of a large saucepan and cover with cold water by at least 2 inches (5 cm). Bring the water to a boil and just as it starts to boil, take the saucepan off the heat. Let sit, covered, for 15 minutes. Drain the eggs and run under cold water to stop the cooking. Peel the eggs. They can be refrigerated until ready to use.

3. Add the mayonnaise, mustard, and salt and pepper to taste and blend into a smooth, spreadable filling mixture.

4. With a small spoon or a pastry bag, fill the egg halves with the yolk mixture. Garnish with a dash of paprika on each egg and serve.

2. Slice the eggs in half widthwise. Scoop the yolks from the eggs into a bowl and mash them with a fork or large spoon.

CRUNCHY ROASTED CHICKPEAS

These spiced oven-roasted chickpeas will assuage your craving for a crunchy salty snack in a very healthful, and yet still satisfying, way. They also make a wonderful crunchy addition to a salad or a mixed-nut bowl.

HERE'S WHAT YOU NEED

1 can (15 ounces, or 425 g) of chickpeas
2 teaspoons salt
1 teaspoon ground black pepper
½ teaspoon garlic powder
¼ teaspoon cayenne pepper (optional)
2 tablespoons (28 ml) olive oil

HERE'S WHAT YOU GET

ABOUT 2 CUPS (425 G) OF SPICY, CRUNCHY CHICKPEAS

Variations

Add ½ teaspoon of curry powder and ½ teaspoon of ground cumin to the spice mixture.

Make them sweet: Skip the salt, pepper, garlic, and cayenne. Roast the chickpeas with olive oil only and then stir them together with 1 teaspoon of sugar and ½ teaspoon of ground cinnamon after they come out of the oven.

HERE'S WHAT YOU DO

1. Preheat the oven to 400°F (200°C, or gas mark 6). In a colander, rinse and drain the chickpeas.

3. Add the salt, pepper, garlic powder, cayenne (if desired), and the olive oil. Stir to coat the chickpeas with the oil and spices.

4. Transfer to a baking sheet and bake for 30 to 40 minutes until crispy and golden. Check frequently after the 25-minute mark and stir as needed to make sure the chickpeas don't burn. Serve at room temperature.

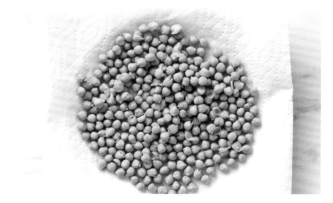

2. Transfer the chickpeas to a plate lined with paper towels and pat as much moisture as possible from the chickpeas. Transfer the dry chickpeas to a bowl.

TERIYAKI PARTY WINGS

Chicken wings seem to be ever increasing in popularity, and your friends will love you for serving them. The saucing options are infinite, but with a classic prepared teriyaki sauce, these oven-baked wings couldn't be simpler.

HERE'S WHAT YOU NEED

3 pounds (1.4 kg) chicken wings, split at the joint and wingtips removed
2 cups (475 g) prepared teriyaki marinade
Nonstick cooking spray
3 scallions, chopped

HERE'S WHAT YOU GET

6 TO 8 CRISPY, SAUCY SERVINGS

A TASTY TIP Look for a good-quality reduced-sodium teriyaki marinade. The wings will still have loads of flavor and will be a bit healthier.

HERE'S WHAT YOU DO

1. In a very large resealable plastic bag (or two), combine the wings and the marinade. Squish the bag(s) a bit to make sure the wings are evenly coated. Refrigerate for at least 4 hours or up to overnight.

3. Remove the pan from the oven and, using tongs, turn each wing over. Return the pan to the oven and bake for 20 to 25 minutes more until the wings are crispy.

4. Arrange the wings on a large plate or platter, sprinkle with the scallions, and serve hot.

2. When ready to bake the wings, preheat the oven to 400°F (200°C, or gas mark 6). Let the bag of wings sit at room temperature for 20 to 30 minutes. Line a baking sheet with aluminum foil and spray the foil evenly with nonstick cooking spray. Arrange the wings in an even layer on the foil. Bake for 20 minutes.

GARLICKY WHITE BEAN DIP

Using canned beans makes this dip a snap to prepare. Cannellini beans have a nice creamy texture, but you can really use any white bean, including Great Northern or navy beans. Besides the crackers, you could serve this with slices of French baguette, pita chips, or fresh vegetables cut into sticks, such as carrots, celery, and zucchini.

HERE'S WHAT YOU NEED

1 can (15 ounces, or 425 g) of cannellini beans, rinsed and drained
2 garlic cloves, minced
¼ cup (15 g) chopped fresh parsley
1 teaspoon salt, plus more as needed
1 teaspoon ground black pepper, plus more as needed
¼ cup (60 ml) olive oil
Your favorite crackers, for serving

HERE'S WHAT YOU GET

1½ CUPS (112 G) OF GARLICKY DIP

A TASTY TIP Using the food processor makes a very smooth dip. For a more home-style, chunkier bean dip, you could mash the beans by hand using a potato masher or a large fork.

HERE'S WHAT YOU DO

1. In a food processor, purée the beans and garlic until smooth.

3. With the food processor running on low speed, slowly pour the olive oil through the feed tube, processing until the dip is emulsified and thick.

2. Add the parsley, salt, and pepper to the puréed beans and process again until everything is thoroughly combined.

4. Transfer the bean dip to a serving bowl, taste, and season with more salt and pepper, if you like.

5. Serve with your favorite crackers for dipping.

NEVER-SOGGY NACHOS

The key to successful nachos is even layering of all the ingredients so that you don't end up with lots of chips with no toppings and a bunch of chips that are soggy from too much topping. These nachos have chopped avocado baked right in, but if you like guac, feel free to serve that up on the side, too, along with the sour cream.

HERE'S WHAT YOU NEED

1 can (15 ounces, or 425 g) of black beans
1 large bag (approximately 16 ounces, or 455 g) of tortilla chips
1 jar (16 ounces, or 455 g) of your favorite salsa
1 cup (180 g) chopped tomatoes
1 avocado, pitted, peeled, and diced
¼ cup (34 g) chopped pickled jalapeño peppers
½ cup (50 g) chopped canned black olives
¼ cup (40 g) chopped red onion
2 cups (225 g) shredded Cheddar cheese
Sour cream, for serving (optional)

HERE'S WHAT YOU GET

1 GIANT NACHO PLATTER, TO SERVE 4 TO 6

A TASTY TIP If you like, add cooked shredded chicken, pulled pork, or leftover beef chili when you are layering the nachos.

HERE'S WHAT YOU DO

1. Preheat the oven to 350°F (180°C, or gas mark 4). In a colander, rinse and drain the black beans. Layer half of the tortilla chips on a large baking sheet. Sprinkle with 1 cup (260 g) of the salsa.

3. Repeat the layering with the remaining tortilla chips and the rest of the ingredients in the same order, finishing with the cheese on top.

4. Bake for 15 to 20 minutes until the cheese is melted and all the ingredients are warmed through. Serve the nachos with sour cream on the side, if desired.

2. Sprinkle half of each of the ingredients over the salsa: beans, tomatoes, avocado, jalapeños, olives, onions, and Cheddar cheese.

SPINACH PARTY POPPERS

These savory and healthy bite-size party poppers will look like you put a lot more effort into them than you did. And they will make your vegetarian friends very happy. If you prefer, you could serve them with a Parmesan-peppercorn dressing rather than the honey Dijon mustard.

HERE'S WHAT YOU NEED

¼ cup (28 g) panko

1½ cups (150 g) grated Parmesan cheese, divided

2 packages (10 ounces, or 280 g each) of frozen spinach, cooked and well drained

2 cups (150 g) herb-seasoned stuffing mix

3 large eggs, lightly beaten

½ cup (1 stick, or 112 g) unsalted butter, softened

1 teaspoon salt

½ teaspoon ground black pepper

4 scallions, chopped

Honey Dijon mustard, for serving

HERE'S WHAT YOU GET

ABOUT 80 BITE-SIZE POPPERS

A TASTY TIP Make sure the spinach is very well drained and squeezed dry of water so that your party bites will be light and fluffy.

HERE'S WHAT YOU DO

1. Preheat the oven to 350°F (180°C, or gas mark 4). Line two large baking sheets with parchment paper. In a shallow bowl, mix the panko with ½ cup (50 g) of the Parmesan. Set aside.

2. In a large bowl, combine the spinach, stuffing mix, remaining 1 cup (100 g) of Parmesan, eggs, butter, salt, pepper, and scallions. Mix thoroughly to combine.

3. Roll the mixture into 1-inch (2.5 cm) balls.

4. Roll each ball in the panko-Parmesan mixture. Place on the prepared baking sheets and place the baking sheets in the freezer for 20 minutes to firm up the spinach balls.

5. Bake the spinach balls for 10 to 15 minutes until heated through and the coating is beginning to brown. Serve the poppers with the honey Dijon mustard on the side for dipping.

CRISPY BAKED CHICKEN NUGGETS

These highly seasoned nuggets are super-flavorful, and baking them instead of frying gives them a nice crunch without making them greasy. If you've got a crowd coming over, you'll want to double the recipe for sure. Don't forget to set out several different dipping sauces.

HERE'S WHAT YOU NEED

Nonstick cooking spray

1 cup (120 g) all-purpose flour

1 teaspoon garlic powder

1 teaspoon onion powder

1 teaspoon salt

1 teaspoon ground black pepper

2 large eggs, beaten with 1 tablespoon (15 ml) water

1 cup (115 g) Italian-style seasoned breadcrumbs

¼ cup (25 g) grated Parmesan or Pecorino cheese

1 pound (455 g) boneless, skinless chicken breast, cut into 1½-inch (3.8 cm) pieces

Dipping sauces of choice, such as honey mustard, barbecue sauce, sweet chili sauce, or ketchup

HERE'S WHAT YOU GET

4 APPETIZER SERVINGS

HERE'S WHAT YOU DO

1. Preheat the oven to 400°F (200°C, or gas mark 6). Line a baking sheet with parchment paper and spray with nonstick cooking spray. In a large resealable plastic bag, mix the flour, garlic powder, onion powder, salt, and pepper. Place the beaten eggs in a shallow bowl. Combine the breadcrumbs and cheese in another shallow bowl.

2. Add the chicken pieces to the bag with the flour, seal the bag, and shake until the chicken pieces are evenly coated with the flour mixture. Dip each piece of chicken into the egg wash, let any excess fall back into the bowl, and then transfer the pieces to the bowl with the breadcrumbs to coat them.

3. Arrange the nuggets on the prepared baking sheet.

4. Bake for 20 to 30 minutes, turning the nuggets over halfway through the baking time.

5. Serve hot, with your favorite dipping sauces.

HOT AND CHEESY ARTICHOKE DIP

It's not a party without hot artichoke dip, right? Seriously, sometimes there is a very good reason why a classic is considered a classic. Here is a case in point.

HERE'S WHAT YOU NEED

1 package (8 ounces, or 225 g) of cream cheese, softened
1 can (14 ounces, or 390 g) of artichoke hearts, drained and chopped
1 cup (115 g) shredded Cheddar cheese
½ cup (50 g) grated Parmesan cheese
½ cup (115 g) mayonnaise
1 teaspoon grated lemon zest
1 tablespoon (15 ml) fresh lemon juice
3 scallions, thinly sliced
¼ teaspoon cayenne pepper (optional)
Pita chips, crackers, or sturdy potato chips, for serving

HERE'S WHAT YOU GET

6 TO 8 WARM, CREAMY SERVINGS

A TASTY TIP You can use frozen artichoke hearts in this dip instead of the canned. Just be sure to thaw completely, pat them dry, and chop them before adding them to the bowl with the cream cheese.

HERE'S WHAT YOU DO

1. Preheat the oven to 375°F (190°C, or gas mark 5). In a large bowl, mix the cream cheese and artichoke hearts with a spatula or fork until well combined and the cream cheese is smooth.

3. Transfer the dip mixture to a 9-inch pie (23 cm) plate or gratin dish.

4. Bake for 20 to 25 minutes until bubbly and lightly browned around the edges. Dig in, directly from the dish, while still warm.

2. Add both cheeses, the mayonnaise, lemon zest and juice, scallions, and cayenne (if desired) and use a spatula to thoroughly blend everything together.

PANKO POPCORN SHRIMP

Sustainable wild shrimp are a little more expensive but are better (for you and the earth) than farmed shrimp. You can often find good deals on bags of frozen shrimp, and since wild shrimp is typically flash-frozen right on the boat, you aren't sacrificing any of that great shrimpy flavor by purchasing frozen.

HERE'S WHAT YOU NEED

1 cup (120 g) all-purpose flour
2 tablespoons (16 g) cornstarch
2 teaspoons dried oregano
2 teaspoons salt
2 teaspoons garlic powder
2 teaspoons paprika
1 teaspoon cayenne pepper
2 large eggs, lightly beaten with 2 tablespoons (28 ml) milk
1 cup (115 g) plain breadcrumbs
1 cup (112 g) panko
1 pound (455 g) medium shrimp (41/50), peeled, deveined, and patted dry
Vegetable oil, as needed
Lemon wedges, for serving
Cocktail or tartar sauce, for serving

HERE'S WHAT YOU GET

6 TO 8 POPPABLE SERVINGS

HERE'S WHAT YOU DO

1. In a large bowl, mix the flour, cornstarch, oregano, salt, garlic powder, paprika, and cayenne.

2. Place the egg-milk mixture in a shallow bowl.

4. Dredge the shrimp in the flour. Dip into the egg mixture to coat, letting any excess drip back into the bowl. Then, dredge the shrimp in the breadcrumb-panko mixture.

3. Mix the breadcrumbs and panko in another shallow bowl.

5. Heat 2 tablespoons (28 ml) of vegetable oil in a large nonstick skillet over medium-high heat. Sauté the shrimp until nice and crispy, 1 to 2 minutes per side. Work in batches so as not to overcrowd the pan, adding more oil to the pan as needed. Drain the shrimp on paper towels as you finish each batch.

6. Serve the shrimp with lemon wedges for squeezing on top and cocktail or tartar sauce for dipping.

ZESTY MARINATED OLIVES

Homemade marinated olives will score you major style points when you're entertaining friends. You can tell them it's your own secret recipe. This makes a big batch, which will keep in the fridge for a very long time, but you can cut the ingredients in half to make only 2 cups (340 g), if you prefer.

HERE'S WHAT YOU NEED

4 cups (680 g) assorted green and black olives, such as Nicoise, Kalamata, Manzanilla, Picholine, etc.

Grated zest of ½ of an orange

Grated zest of ½ of a lemon

3 garlic cloves, minced

3 tablespoons (5 g) chopped fresh rosemary

Pinch of cayenne pepper

Salt and ground black pepper to taste

¼ to ⅓ cup (60 to 80 ml) olive oil (enough to coat the olives)

HERE'S WHAT YOU GET

AT LEAST 16 SERVINGS OF OLIVES

A TASTY TIP Vary the seasonings to suit your tastes. You could use crushed red pepper instead of the cayenne, or use oregano instead of the rosemary, or add a little wine vinegar along with the oil . . . .

HERE'S WHAT YOU DO

1. Put the olives in a colander and rinse quickly under cold water. Shake to dry them a bit. Transfer the olives to a large bowl.

2. Add the citrus zests, garlic, rosemary, cayenne, and salt and black pepper to taste. Mix well to evenly coat the olives with the seasonings.

3. Add the olive oil and toss to combine well and coat the olives with the oil.

4. Cover and let the olives marinate at room temperature for at least 3 hours before serving. You can refrigerate the olives in an airtight container, but let them come to room temperature before serving.

SOUPS, SALADS, and SANDWICHES

CREAM OF MUSHROOM SOUP

Use whatever mushrooms you like in this soup: Everyday button mushrooms all by themselves make a fabulous soup, or use a mixture of exotic wild mushrooms to make an elegant, company-worthy cream soup.

HERE'S WHAT YOU NEED

4 tablespoons (56 g) unsalted butter
1 tablespoon (15 ml) olive oil
1 cup (160 g) chopped yellow onion
1 teaspoon salt
½ teaspoon ground black pepper
1½ pounds (680 g) mushrooms (such as button, cremini, portobello, and shiitake), sliced or chopped (about 8 cups)
1 quart (950 ml) chicken or vegetable broth
1 teaspoon dried thyme
½ cup (120 ml) heavy cream
1 cup (235 ml) milk

HERE'S WHAT YOU GET

4 TO 6 SMOOTH, CREAMY BOWLS OF SOUP

HERE'S WHAT YOU DO

1. In a large stockpot, melt the butter and olive oil together over medium-high heat. Add the onion and sauté until softened, about 5 minutes. Add the salt and pepper.

2. Add the mushrooms and sauté for 10 to 15 minutes until they begin to brown.

4. Strain the mushrooms and other solids from the stockpot, reserving the liquid. Set aside 1 cup (235 ml) of the liquid and put the rest of it back into the pot.

3. Add the broth and thyme to the pot. Bring to a boil and then reduce the heat and simmer for 20 minutes.

5. In a food processor or blender, purée the mushrooms with the 1 cup (235 ml) of liquid until smooth. Add this mixture to the stockpot and stir to mix it with the broth.

6. Slowly add the cream and milk to the pot and heat through without letting the soup come to a boil. Serve the soup hot.

TUSCAN VEGETABLE SOUP

There are dozens of kinds of vegetable-and-bean soups in Italian cuisine. What's the signature style of a Tuscan soup? Usually, it's the use of white beans and ample greens, such as kale or spinach. Think about serving this with some crusty Italian bread on the side.

HERE'S WHAT YOU NEED

2 tablespoons (28 ml) olive oil
1 cup (130 g) diced carrots
1 celery stalk, diced
1 medium yellow onion, diced
2 garlic cloves, minced
1 large tomato, chopped
1½ quarts (1.4 L) vegetable or chicken broth
1 teaspoon dried oregano
1 teaspoon dried basil
1 cup (120 g) diced zucchini
1 can (15 ounces, or 425 g) of white beans,
  rinsed and drained
4 cups loosely packed (280 g) baby kale
  or (120 g) baby spinach, or a mixture
Salt and ground black pepper to taste
Grated Parmesan cheese, for serving

HERE'S WHAT YOU GET

4 HEARTY AND WARMING BOWLS OF SOUP

HERE'S WHAT YOU DO

1. Heat the olive oil in a large stockpot. Add the carrots, celery, and onion. Cook until soft, about 10 minutes. Add the garlic and cook until fragrant, about 1 minute.

3. Add the zucchini and simmer for 5 minutes. Then add the beans and simmer for 5 minutes more.

2. Add the tomato, broth, and herbs and bring to a boil. Reduce the heat to low and simmer, covered, for 10 to 15 minutes.

4. Remove the soup from the heat and stir in the kale or spinach. Cover and let sit for 10 minutes. Taste the soup and season with salt and pepper if needed.

5. Serve hot and top each individual serving with the Parmesan.

VICHYSSOISE

Vichyssoise—potato and leek cream soup—is traditionally served cold as an appetizer or first course, but there's no reason you can't have a bigger bowl as a lunch or dinner all on its own. Julia Child tells us that despite the fancy French name, this soup is an American invention.

HERE'S WHAT YOU NEED

2 tablespoons (28 ml) olive oil

1 tablespoon (14 g) unsalted butter

4 cups (356 g) sliced leeks, white and light green parts only, washed clean of sand and dirt (about 3 medium leeks)

1 medium yellow onion, chopped

1½ pounds (680 g) Yukon Gold potatoes, peeled and cut into 1-inch (2.5 cm) chunks

1½ quarts (1.4 L) chicken broth

1 cup (235 ml) heavy cream

Salt and ground black pepper to taste

HERE'S WHAT YOU GET

4 MAIN, OR 8 SMALL FIRST-COURSE SERVINGS OF REFRESHING CHILLED SOUP

HERE'S WHAT YOU DO

1. In a stockpot over low heat, heat the olive oil and butter together. Add the leeks and onion and sauté until softened and wilted, about 5 minutes.

A TASTY TIP You can also serve this soup hot, for a warming winter meal.

2. Add the potatoes and mix them into the ingredients.

4. When cool, transfer the soup in batches to a food processor or blender and purée until completely smooth. Or use an immersion blender right in the stockpot. Transfer the soup to the refrigerator for at least 4 hours to chill.

3. Add the broth. Bring to a boil and then reduce the heat, cover, and simmer until the potatoes are cooked through and soft, 20 to 30 minutes. Remove from the heat and let the soup cool to room temperature (about 1 hour).

5. After the soup has chilled, add the heavy cream, stirring to combine.

6. Taste the soup, season with salt and pepper as desired, and serve cold.

CREAM OF TOMATO SOUP

Cream of tomato soup with a grilled cheese sandwich on the side? Yes, please! This is an Italian-style creamy tomato soup, so please consider making your grilled cheese sandwich with provolone or mozzarella cheese.

HERE'S WHAT YOU NEED

3 tablespoons (45 ml) olive oil
2½ cups (400 g) diced yellow onions
3 cloves garlic, minced
3 pounds (1.4 kg) tomatoes, cored and chopped
1½ teaspoons salt , plus more as needed
½ teaspoon dried basil
½ teaspoon dried oregano
2 cups (475 ml) vegetable broth
Ground black pepper to taste
1 cup (235 ml) heavy cream or half-and-half
¼ cup (10 g) chopped fresh basil,
   plus more for garnish (optional)

HERE'S WHAT YOU GET

4 TO 6 BRIGHT-TASTING BOWLS

HERE'S WHAT YOU DO

1. In a large stockpot, heat the olive oil over medium heat. Add the onions and cook until softened, about 5 minutes. Add the garlic and cook for a minute or so more.

2. Add the tomatoes, salt, basil, and oregano to the pot. Bring to a boil and then reduce the heat and simmer, covered, for 45 minutes. Remove the cover and cook for 15 minutes more. Add the broth and season with pepper to taste. Remove from the heat and let cool for 1 hour.

4. Pour the blended mixture through a fine-mesh strainer into a bowl, pressing on the solids to release all of their juices. Discard the pulp and seeds left in the strainer.

3. Once cool, transfer in batches to a food processor or blender and purée until smooth. Or use an immersion blender right in the stockpot.

5. Return the soup to the stockpot and add the cream. Slowly reheat the soup, making sure it does not come to a boil. Taste and add more salt and pepper, if desired.

6. Stir in the fresh basil. Serve the soup warm.

ASIAN-INSPIRED CUCUMBER SALAD

You can make this salad a bit ahead of time, but just be aware that the cucumbers will soften in the fridge and the dressing flavors will become a bit more intense. Serving it right away preserves the crispness of the cukes. This salad is great alongside teriyaki grilled chicken or salmon.

HERE'S WHAT YOU NEED

2 English cucumbers
4 scallions, thinly sliced
1 tablespoon (15 g) Dijon mustard
1 tablespoon (15 ml) soy sauce
2 teaspoons red wine vinegar
2 teaspoons rice vinegar
½ cup (120 ml) toasted sesame oil
¼ cup (60 ml) olive oil
1 tablespoon (8 g) sesame seeds, toasted

HERE'S WHAT YOU GET

4 TO 6 LIGHT AND FRESH SERVINGS

HERE'S WHAT YOU DO

1. Pat the cucumbers dry, if necessary. Slice each cucumber in half lengthwise and then slice each half again horizontally. You will have 8 pieces.

2. Using a teaspoon, scoop the seeds from the cucumber pieces.

4. In a separate bowl, whisk together the mustard, soy sauce, and both vinegars until combined. Slowly add both oils, whisking until the dressing thickens and emulsifies.

3. Cut each cucumber piece into slices ⅓-inch (8 mm) thick. Transfer the cucumber slices to a bowl and add the scallions.

5. Pour the dressing over the cucumber slices and the scallions and toss well to combine.

6. Sprinkle the cucumber salad with the sesame seeds and serve immediately.

MULTICOLORED TORTELLINI SALAD

Because you can buy already cooked cheese tortellini in any supermarket, this colorful and healthy salad, substantial enough to be a main course, takes just minutes to put together.

HERE'S WHAT YOU NEED

1 pound (455 g) cooked cheese tortellini
2 tablespoons (28 ml) olive oil
1 large red bell pepper, diced
1 large or 2 small scallions, thinly sliced
1 celery stalk, diced
1 cup (225 g) sliced pepperoni, each slice cut into quarters
½ to 1 cup (120 to 240 g) Parmesan peppercorn or ranch dressing

HERE'S WHAT YOU GET

4 COLORFUL AND NUTRITIOUS SALAD SERVINGS

A TASTY TIP Most stores have at least three colors of precooked cheese tortellini: a plain white pasta, a green pasta (spinach makes it green), and a red pasta (tomatoes make it red). Try whichever variety you like in this salad—and also look for different fillings in addition to the cheese, such as pesto or meat.

HERE'S WHAT YOU DO

1. In a large bowl, toss the cooked tortellini with the olive oil.

3. Toss in the pepperoni and then add the dressing and toss everything to mix it all up.

4. Serve the tortellini at room temperature or chilled.

2. Add the red bell pepper, scallions, and celery.

NiCOiSE SALAD

Salade Nicoise is a French composed (or arranged) salad that comes from Nice, in the South of France. We Americans have changed it a bit to suit our tastes, adding cooked potatoes and green beans, leaving out the traditional anchovies, and so on. With a baguette, this substantial salad is a meal.

HERE'S WHAT YOU NEED

1 pound (455 g) red potatoes, cut into ⅓-inch (8 mm) slices

8 ounces (225 g) green beans, trimmed

1 tablespoon (15 g) Dijon mustard

2 tablespoons (28 ml) red wine vinegar

¼ cup (60 ml) olive oil

Salt and ground black pepper to taste

2 cans (5 ounces, or 140 g) of tuna packed in olive oil, drained

4 large hardboiled eggs, peeled and quartered

1 pint (475 ml) cherry tomatoes, cut in half

¼ cup (40 g) chopped red onion

½ cup (70 g) pitted black olives (Nicoise or Greek), sliced

¼ cup (15 g) chopped fresh parsley

HERE'S WHAT YOU GET

4 FLAVOR-PACKED SERVINGS

HERE'S WHAT YOU DO

1. Put the potatoes in a large pot and cover with water. Bring to a boil. Reduce the heat to a simmer and cook for 5 minutes or until the potatoes are fork-tender. Drain and set aside to cool. In a large saucepan, bring water to a boil and cook the green beans for 6 minutes. Rinse under cold water to stop the cooking, drain, and set aside.

2. Make the dressing by whisking the mustard and vinegar together and slowly adding the olive oil, while whisking, until thickened and emulsified. Season with salt and pepper to taste.

4. Put the potatoes on the right side of the platter. Arrange the tomatoes in small piles on either side of the potatoes and green beans.

3. On a large serving platter, arrange your ingredients as follows: Put the tuna in the middle of the platter. Arrange the eggs at each end of the platter. Put the green beans on the left side of the platter.

5. Sprinkle the whole salad with the onions, olives, (2 tablespoons [17 g] of capers if desired), and parsley.

6. Before serving, drizzle the whole salad evenly with the dressing. After you present it, you can gently toss it together, if you like.

OPEN-FACED CROQUE MONSIEUR

Croque monsieur is French for "Mr. Crunch." Ah, those French. The dish originated in French cafés as a quick snack. It can be baked or griddled and is often served closed up, like a regular sandwich, but this version is open-faced. Top it with a fried egg, and you can call it *croque madame*, or "Mrs. Crunch."

HERE'S WHAT YOU NEED

4 slices (½ inch, or 1.3 cm thick) rustic country bread (such as a boule)
4 tablespoons (60 g) Dijon mustard
8 slices of country ham, jambon de Paris, or Black Forest ham
8 slices of Gruyère, Emmenthaler, or Swiss cheese
Cornichons or your favorite pickles, for serving

HERE'S WHAT YOU GET

2 BIG SERVINGS OR 4 SMALLER ONES

A TASTY TIP Cornichons are tart, tiny whole gherkin pickles that are often served with pâté. They are worth finding because they are so delicious, but any pickle would be good here.

HERE'S WHAT YOU DO

1. Preheat the oven to 350°F (180°C, or gas mark 4). Place the 4 slices of bread on a baking sheet. Spread 1 tablespoon (15 g) of the mustard over each bread slice.

3. Top the ham with 2 slices of cheese.

2. Top each bread slice with 2 slices of ham.

4. Bake in the oven for 10 to 15 minutes until the cheese is bubbly and starting to turn golden.

5. Serve the open-face sandwiches hot, with cornichons or your favorite pickles.

GRIDDLED THAI CHICKEN SANDWICHES

These hearty griddled Thai-inspired sandwiches make for a really satisfying meal all on their own. If you like, make a big salad or some soup, cut the sandwiches in half, and serve four people instead of two people.

HERE'S WHAT YOU NEED

¼ cup (60 g) mayonnaise

2 tablespoons (32 g) store-bought peanut sauce, plus more for serving (optional)

4 thick slices of country bread or 1 (8-inch, or 20 cm) ciabatta or sub roll

8 ounces (225 g) rotisserie chicken or leftover cooked chicken

14 thin slices of English cucumber

6 slices of tomato

6 large leaves Thai or regular basil

4 slices of Cheddar cheese

2 tablespoons (28 g) unsalted butter, softened

2 tablespoons (28 ml) olive oil

Sweet chili sauce, for serving (optional)

HERE'S WHAT YOU GET

2 LARGE SANDWICHES OR 4 SMALLER ONES

HERE'S WHAT YOU DO

1. Mix the mayonnaise and peanut sauce together in a small bowl. Build the sandwiches as follow: Spread 1½ tablespoons (25 g) of the peanut mayonnaise on each piece of bread or on both sides of the cut roll. Layer the chicken, cucumber slices, tomato slices, basil leaves, and Cheddar cheese slices evenly over the bread.

2. Top the cheese with the remaining bread slices or the top half of the roll. Spread 1½ teaspoons of butter on top of each bread slice or 1 tablespoon (14 g) of butter over the top of the roll.

4. Spread the remaining butter on top of both sandwiches or on top of the roll and carefully flip the sandwiches over.

3. Heat the olive oil in a large (enough to hold both sandwiches) griddle pan or nonstick skillet over medium heat. Carefully put the sandwiches into skillet, buttered-side down, and cook for 3 minutes or until golden brown.

5. Top the sandwiches with a heavy cast iron pan (or bacon press if you have one) to press the sandwiches down. Cook for 5 minutes more until golden brown and the cheese is fully melted.

6. Serve with extra peanut sauce and sweet chili sauce for dipping, if desired.

KICKIN' QUESADILLAS

For the best quesadillas, make sure to shred your meat fillings. There's nothing worse than pulling out a big chunk of chicken in one bite and then having none left in your quesadilla. Likewise, if you use veggies, chop them into small pieces and pat them dry of excess moisture so that you don't end up with soggy quesadillas.

HERE'S WHAT YOU NEED

1 package (8 ounces, 225 g) of cream
  cheese, softened
2 cups (225 g) shredded Cheddar cheese
2 tablespoons (12 g) chopped scallion
1 teaspoon dried oregano
1 teaspoon ground cumin
1 teaspoon chili powder
8 taco-size flour tortillas (6 inches, or 15 cm)
1 cup filling, such as (238 g) shredded cooked
  chicken or beef, (247 g) leftover chili, (156 g)
  chopped cooked broccoli, any leftover cooked
  vegetables, or a mixture of some or all
Vegetable oil, as needed
Chopped avocado, salsa, and lime wedges,
  for serving

HERE'S WHAT YOU GET

4 TACO-SIZE QUESADILLAS TO SNACK ON

A TASTY TIP Corn and chipotle peppers with a bit of the adobo sauce also make a great filling combo— or zucchini and jalapeños. There are so many possibilities.

HERE'S WHAT YOU DO

1. Preheat the oven to 200°F (93°C). In a bowl, mix the cream cheese, Cheddar cheese, scallion, oregano, cumin, and chili powder to a smooth, spreadable consistency.

3. Spread ¼ cup (weight will vary) of your chosen filling on top of the cheese mixture. Top the filling with another tortilla.

2. Spread 2 tablespoons (28 g) of the cheese mixture evenly over 4 of the tortillas.

4. Heat 2 teaspoons of vegetable oil in a nonstick skillet over medium-low heat. Cook the quesadillas, one at a time, for 1½ minutes on each side until crispy and golden. Add more oil to the skillet as needed. Transfer the finished quesadillas to the oven to keep warm.

5. When ready to serve, cut each tortilla into 4 wedges and serve with sliced avocado, salsa, and lime wedges.

PASTAS, GRAINS, and BEANS

NAAN MINI PIZZAS

People make mini pizzas using all sorts of things as the base, like bagel halves or pita breads or English muffins, in place of the pizza dough. My favorite is naan, which is a common bread in Asia, especially India. It has a rich and even creamy flavor because it is usually made with milk or yogurt. It's easy to find naan in supermarkets or Asian markets.

HERE'S WHAT YOU NEED

4 individual-size naan bread rounds
½ cup (130 g) prepared basil pesto
1 cup (245 g) tomato sauce or pizza sauce
Your favorite toppings, such as sliced pepperoni, shredded cooked chicken, crumbled bacon, sliced bell peppers, sliced mushrooms, black olives, etc.
1 to 2 cups (115 to 230 g) shredded mozzarella cheese

HERE'S WHAT YOU GET

4 EASY-TO-MAKE INDIVIDUAL PIZZAS

A TASTY TIP Naan breads come in many different sizes, but 6 to 8 inches (15 to 20 cm) in diameter is ideal here. If the ones you find are much bigger than that, you could cut them in half—or you could just use a little more of all the other ingredients!

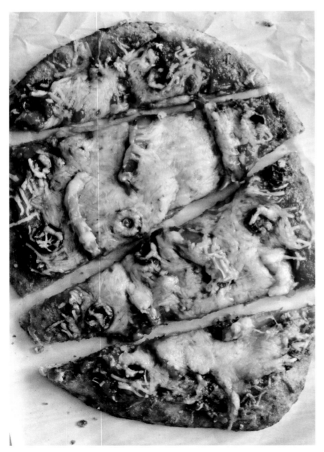

HERE'S WHAT YOU DO

1. Preheat the oven to 400°F (200°C, or gas mark 6). Place the naan breads on a baking sheet and use a spoon to spread the pesto evenly over them.

3. Sprinkle your favorite toppings on top of the tomato sauce.

2. Spread the tomato sauce evenly over the pesto.

4. Distribute the shredded mozzarella evenly on top of the pizzas.

5. Bake for about 10 minutes or until the cheese is melted. Remove from the oven and let rest for 3 minutes. Cut the naan pizzas into wedges or slices and serve.

PASTA FRITTATA

This breakfast-for-dinner mash-up is one for the ages. A frittata is simply a baked Italian version of an omelet, and adding leftover cooked pasta is actually a time-honored, authentic Italian tradition. Spaghetti is traditionally used, but you can use other shapes instead. Feel free to also add leftover cooked vegetables, chopped up. If you would like an eggier frittata, you can use eight eggs.

HERE'S WHAT YOU NEED

2 tablespoons (28 g) unsalted butter, divided
6 large eggs
⅓ cup (33 g) grated Parmesan cheese
¼ cup (60 ml) milk
4 cups (560 g) cooked spaghetti
  (8 ounces, or 225 g uncooked)
Salt and ground black pepper to taste
Chopped tomatoes, for serving
Chopped fresh basil, for garnish

HERE'S WHAT YOU GET

4 TO 6 PUFFY, GOLDEN SERVINGS

A TASTY TIP You don't necessarily have to use plain pasta in this frittata. If you have leftover sauced pasta, warm it slightly in the microwave and then lift it out of the sauce. That way, you won't have a liquidy frittata that falls apart. And you can use the leftover sauce as a topping.

HERE'S WHAT YOU DO

1. Preheat the oven to 350°F (180°C, or gas mark 4). Butter a 10-inch (25 cm) cast iron skillet with 1 tablespoon (14 g) of the butter.

3. Transfer the mixture to the skillet. Cut the remaining 1 tablespoon (14 g) of butter into small pieces and dot the top of the frittata. Bake for 10 minutes. After 10 minutes, take the skillet out of the oven and stir the mixture slightly.

2. In a large bowl, beat the eggs well. Add salt and pepper to taste. Add the Parmesan, milk, and pasta, stirring to coat the pasta with the wet ingredients.

4. Return the frittata to the oven and bake for 10 to 15 minutes more or until the frittata is puffy and golden. Let the frittata sit for a few minutes to cool and set and then unmold it into a serving dish (or serve directly from the skillet, if you like).

5. Top with the tomatoes and sprinkle with the basil. Serve warm.

NEAPOLITAN CALZONES

A calzone is basically a portable pizza, invented—just like pizza—in Naples, Italy. These oversize "hot pockets" are even easier to eat on the go than pizza, and they also freeze really well, so you can make a double batch and have grab-and-go work lunches galore.

HERE'S WHAT YOU NEED

1 pound (455 g) pizza dough, at room temperature
Flour, for rolling the pizza dough
8 ounces (225 g) ricotta cheese
6 ounces (170 g) fresh mozzarella cheese, cubed
½ cup (50 g) grated Parmesan cheese, divided
1 large egg
4 ounces (115 g) ham or salami, chopped
1 large egg, beaten with 1 tablespoon (15 ml) milk to make an egg wash
Your favorite tomato sauce, warmed, for serving

HERE'S WHAT YOU GET

4 HEALTHY BUT HEARTY CALZONES

HERE'S WHAT YOU DO

1. Preheat the oven to 375°F (190°C, or gas mark 5). Line a baking sheet with parchment paper. Cut the dough into 4 equal pieces. On a floured surface, roll each piece into a 6- to 7-inch (15 to 18 cm) round.

Variation

For a vegetarian calzone, just leave out the ham or salami. Maybe sub in a vegetable, like roasted eggplant, roasted red peppers, or cooked and well-drained spinach.

2. In a bowl, mix the ricotta, mozzarella, and ¼ cup (25 g) of the Parmesan. Break the egg into the cheese mixture and carefully mix in with a fork until evenly combined. Fold in the ham or salami.

4. Place the calzones on the prepared baking sheet. With a knife or a pair of scissors, cut 3 small holes in the top of each calzone to let steam escape.

3. Divide the mixture equally among the dough rounds, leaving about a ½-inch (1.3 cm) border free around the edges. Brush the edges of the dough rounds with some of the egg wash and fold each dough round into a half-moon, making sure to seal the edges very carefully by pinching the dough together.

5. Brush each calzone with the remaining egg wash and sprinkle the tops with the remaining ¼ cup (25 g) of Parmesan.

6. Bake on the middle rack of the oven for 20 minutes, rotating the pan halfway through the baking time. Serve the calzones hot or warm, with your favorite tomato sauce on the side for dipping.

SPAGHETTI CARBONARA

Pasta carbonara can inspire very strong opinions. There's a lot of debate about what makes an "authentic" pasta carbonara. Onions or not? Cream or not? What kind of meat to use? Tempers may flare. But put your faith in this delicious version, and you'll be able to stand strong in your convictions.

HERE'S WHAT YOU NEED

1 pound (455 g) spaghetti
2 tablespoons (28 ml) olive oil
8 slices of bacon, chopped
1 small yellow onion, diced
½ cup (120 ml) chicken broth
2 large eggs
2 large egg yolks
½ cup (50 g) grated Parmesan cheese, plus more for serving
Cracked black pepper to taste
2 tablespoons (8 g) chopped fresh parsley

HERE'S WHAT YOU GET

4 TO 6 RICH, EGGY SERVINGS

HERE'S WHAT YOU DO

1. Bring a large pot of salted water to a boil and cook the pasta.

A TASTY TIP If you can get your hands on guanciale (cured pork jowl) or pancetta (cured Italian bacon), sub in about ½ pound (225 g) of either for the bacon.

2. In the meantime, heat the olive oil in a large, deep skillet over medium heat. Add the bacon and cook until crispy.

4. In a bowl, mix the eggs, egg yolks, and Parmesan. Set aside. When the pasta is done, drain it and mix it into the bacon-onion mixture in the skillet. Turn the heat to low.

3. Add the onion and cook for 2 minutes more. Add the chicken broth and let the liquid cook and reduce for 3 minutes.

5. Working quickly, add the egg mixture to the skillet and stir, making sure the pasta gets completely coated with the sauce.

6. Transfer the pasta to a serving bowl and sprinkle with the cracked black pepper and the parsley. Serve with more Parmesan for topping.

QUINOA PILAF SALAD

Quinoa, the ancient grain of the Incas, has a lot of protein and a rich, nutty flavor, making it a delicious and healthy change of pace from rice in a pilaf. You can make this pilaf salad on a weekend and then keep it in the fridge for quick lunches or side dishes throughout the week ahead.

HERE'S WHAT YOU NEED

1 cup (173 g) quinoa, rinsed and drained
2 cups (475 ml) chicken or vegetable broth
Juice of 1 lime, plus more as needed
¼ cup (60 ml) olive oil
2 teaspoons salt, plus more as needed
1 teaspoon ground black pepper, plus more as needed
1 cup (135 g) diced English or Persian cucumber
¼ cup (23 g) sliced almonds, toasted
¼ cup (40 g) diced red onion
¼ cup (33 g) sliced dried apricots
2 tablespoons (8 g) chopped fresh parsley
3 tablespoons (18 g) chopped fresh mint
½ cup (75 g) crumbled feta cheese

HERE'S WHAT YOU GET

4 TO 6 HEALTHY SERVINGS

A TASTY TIP Quinoa has a natural coating of saponins, a compound that helps to protect the plant against microbes. However, these saponins can have a bitter taste. Some quinoa producers rinse the grain before packaging it, but some don't, so to be on the safe side, rinse and drain your quinoa in a fine-mesh sieve at the outset.

HERE'S WHAT YOU DO

1. In a medium saucepan, bring the quinoa and broth to a boil. Reduce the heat and simmer for 15 minutes.

3. When cooled down, fold in the cucumber, almonds, onion, apricots, parsley, and mint.

2. Transfer the quinoa to a large bowl. Mix in the lime juice, olive oil, salt, and pepper. Let cool to room temperature.

4. Taste the salad for seasoning, adding more salt, pepper, and/or lime juice if desired. Sprinkle with the feta cheese and serve.

YOUR NEW GO-TO MAC AND CHEESE

Forget about all of that boxed macaroni and cheese with the powdery packets. That's kid stuff. Macaroni and cheese is incredibly fast and easy to make from scratch, and it's so much more wholesome that way, too. And yes, it tastes infinitely better to boot.

HERE'S WHAT YOU NEED

1 pound (455 g) small macaroni, cooked accoding to package directions
6 tablespoons (85 g) unsalted butter
6 tablespoons (48 g) all-purpose flour
3 cups (700 ml) milk, plus more if needed
Pinch of ground nutmeg
2 cups (225 g) shredded white Cheddar cheese
Salt and ground black pepper to taste

HERE'S WHAT YOU GET

4 TO 6 GOOEY, CHEESY PORTIONS

Variations

Stir in ½ cup (40 g) of crumbled cooked bacon when you are mixing the pasta and cheese sauce.

Gently fold in 2 cups (290 g) of chopped cooked lobster meat just before serving.

To bake: Preheat the oven to 350°F (180°C, or gas mark 4) and butter a 9 x 13-inch (23 x 33 cm) baking dish. Transfer the mixture to the pan. Sprinkle with 1 cup (115 g) of cheese and ½ cup (60 g) of bread-crumbs. Bake for about 15 minutes until golden.

HERE'S WHAT YOU DO

1. While the pasta cooks, in a saucepan, melt the butter over medium heat until foamy. Add the flour and whisk it in until smooth, cooking and whisking for 2 minutes.

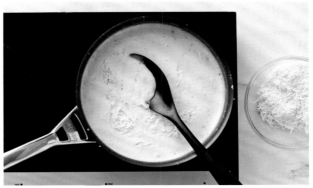

3. When the sauce is thick and, well, saucy, remove the saucepan from the heat and stir in the cheese until melted and smooth. Taste and season with salt and pepper as desired.

2. Slowly pour the milk into the saucepan while still whisking. Reduce the heat to medium and continue whisking until the mixture thickens, about 5 minutes. Add a pinch of nutmeg.

4. When the pasta is done cooking, drain the pasta and return it to the pot. Add the cheese sauce to the pot, stirring to coat the pasta. If it seems a bit too thick, add a bit of milk, stirring to combine and heat it.

5. Serve the mac and cheese immediately.

LOADED STIR-FRIED RICE

Mix up the vegetables you include in this fried rice as you please. Just remember to cut them into small pieces so they cook quickly. Stir-frying is all about the speed! You could add any leftover cooked meat or combo of meats along with the vegetables: chopped-up chicken, beef, or pork, or sliced sausages, or a can of small shrimp.

HERE'S WHAT YOU NEED

4 tablespoons (60 ml) vegetable oil, divided
3 large eggs, lightly beaten
2 garlic cloves, minced
2 tablespoons (12 g) minced or (16 g) grated fresh ginger
5 scallions, chopped, white and green parts separated
1 cup (154 g) corn kernels
1 cup (110 g) grated carrot
4 cups (744 g) cooked white rice
3 tablespoons (45 ml) soy sauce

HERE'S WHAT YOU GET

4 LOADED-UP SERVINGS

HERE'S WHAT YOU DO

1. Heat 2 tablespoons (28 ml) of the vegetable oil in a large nonstick skillet or a wok over medium-high heat. Add the eggs and let cook for about 30 seconds. Flip the eggs over and finish cooking the egg patty until fully cooked, about another 30 seconds.

A TASTY TIP For the lightest, fluffiest fried rice, start with cold cooked rice. Doing that helps keep the rice grains from clumping in the wok and getting mushy.

2. Transfer the egg patty to a cutting board. Chop into 1-inch (2.5 cm) pieces and set aside.

4. Add the whites of the scallions, the corn, carrots, and rice and stir-fry until the vegetables have softened and the rice is heated through, about 5 minutes.

3. Add the remaining 2 tablespoons (30 ml) of oil to the skillet. Add the garlic and ginger and stir-fry for 1 minute.

5. Add the soy sauce, and reserved chopped egg patty and toss to incorporate everything together.

6. Transfer the fried rice to a serving bowl. Sprinkle with the scallion greens and serve.

STEWY LENTILS AND SAUSAGE

This Italian-inspired one-pot dish is flavorful and filling. In keeping with the rustic style, serve it with bits of crusty bread for *fare la scarpetta*, the Italian tradition of making a "little shoe" to sop up every bit of the sauciness in the bottom of the bowl.

HERE'S WHAT YOU NEED

1 tablespoon (15 ml) olive oil
2 pounds (900 g) sweet Italian sausages
2 carrots, peeled and diced
1 medium yellow onion, diced
2 teaspoons salt
1 teaspoon ground black pepper
1 teaspoon dried thyme
1 pound (455 g) lentils, picked through, rinsed, and drained
4 cups (960 ml) beef broth, plus more if needed
Whole-grain mustard, for serving (optional)

HERE'S WHAT YOU GET

4 COUNTRY-STYLE SERVINGS

HERE'S WHAT YOU DO

1. In a Dutch oven, heat the olive oil over medium-high heat. Cook the sausages until they are brown on all sides, 4 to 5 minutes per side. (You don't have to fully cook them at this point.) Remove the sausages from the pot and set aside on a plate. Keep the fat in the pot.

2. Add the carrots, onion, salt, pepper, and thyme to the pot and sauté until the carrots and onions are softened, about 5 minutes.

3. Add the lentils to the pot, stirring to mix them with the vegetables. Add the broth, raise the heat, and bring to a boil.

4. Reduce the heat to a simmer and nestle the sausages into the lentils. Cover and cook for 45 minutes to 1 hour until the lentils are tender and the sausages are fully cooked, adding more broth if it looks like it's getting too dry.

5. Taste, adjust the seasoning as you like, and serve along with whole-grain mustard on the side, if desired.

ALL KINDS OF VEGETABLE DISHES

HAM and CHEESE CAULIFLOWER GRATIN

Cauliflower seems to be having its moment in the sun lately, like kale did a few years back. More and more you're seeing cauliflower "steaks" on restaurant menus, in the entrée section. Personally, we think it's hard to make cauliflower sound appealing to most people when you compare it to a steak. But it really is so yummy, and the cheese, butter, and ham here make it fairly decadent.

HERE'S WHAT YOU NEED

1 medium head cauliflower, cut into 2-inch (5 cm) chunks (8 to 10 cups, or 800 g to 1 kg)

4 tablespoons (55 g) unsalted butter, plus more for preparing the baking dish

¼ cup (31 g) all-purpose flour

3 cups (700 ml) whole milk, warmed

½ teaspoon salt

¼ teaspoon ground black pepper

Pinch of ground nutmeg

1½ cups (173 g) shredded Cheddar cheese, divided

2 cups (300 g) ham cut into 1-inch (2.5 cm) cubes (optional)

HERE'S WHAT YOU GET

6 TO 8 SCOOPS OF CHEESY CAULIFLOWER

HERE'S WHAT YOU DO

1. Preheat the oven to 350°F (180°C, or gas mark 4) and butter a deep 9 x 13-inch (23 x 33 cm) baking dish. Bring a large pot of water to a boil. Drop in the cauliflower, reduce the heat to medium-high, and cook for 8 minutes until fork-tender. Drain the florets in a colander, transfer to a large bowl, and set aside.

2. In the meantime, melt the 4 tablespoons (55 g) of butter in a saucepan over low heat. Add the flour and stir and cook for 2 minutes until the flour is incorporated and the mixture is smooth.

3. Slowly whisk in the warm milk and keep whisking until the sauce thickens, about 5 minutes. Add the salt, pepper, and nutmeg.

4. Take the saucepan off the heat and stir in ½ cup (58 g) of the Cheddar cheese until melted and combined.

5. Slowly pour the sauce mixture into the bowl with the cauliflower and mix it together until the florets are coated with the sauce. Add the ham, if desired, and stir to combine.

6. Transfer the mixture to the prepared baking dish. Sprinkle with the remaining 1 cup (115 g) of cheese.

7. Bake for 20 to 30 minutes until the top is bubbly and the cheese is golden. Serve hot.

TWICE-BAKED STUFFED RUSSETS

Think of these stuffed potatoes as a base recipe, a palette for all kinds of additional mix-ins and toppings. As is, it's a great side dish for 8 people. Loaded up with veggies, meat, and more, it becomes an awesome weeknight dinner for 4 people.

HERE'S WHAT YOU NEED

4 medium russet potatoes, pricked all over with a fork or paring knife

Olive oil, for brushing

4 tablespoons (55 g) unsalted butter, cut into small pieces

¼ cup (60 g) sour cream

¼ cup (60 ml) heavy cream

2 cups (225 g) shredded Cheddar cheese, divided

HERE'S WHAT YOU GET

8 STUFFED POTATO HALVES

HERE'S WHAT YOU DO

1. Preheat the oven to 400°F (200°C, or gas mark 6). Brush the potatoes with olive oil and place them on a baking sheet and into the oven. Bake for 20 minutes. Turn the potatoes over and bake for 15 to 20 minutes more until tender.

Variations

Add 4 slices of chopped cooked bacon to the potato mixture. Top with chopped chives or scallions before serving.

Add 1 cup (156 g) of cooked broccoli florets to the stuffing mixture.

2. Let the potatoes sit until you can handle them but they are still warm, about 15 minutes. Cut the potatoes in half.

4. Scatter the butter over the warm potato flesh and mix, mashing the butter in to incorporate it. Add the sour cream and heavy cream and stir, basically creating mashed potatoes. Add 1 cup (115 g) of the Cheddar cheese and stir to combine.

3. With a spoon, scoop the potato flesh into a large bowl, being careful not to tear the potato skins, which will be the "shell." Return the scooped-out potatoes halves to the baking sheet.

5. Transfer the mixture to the potato halves, gently stuffing them full without packing the filling too tight. Top them equally with the remaining 1 cup (115 g) of cheese.

6. Transfer the baking sheet to the oven and bake for 25 to 30 minutes until the Cheddar is bubbly and golden. Serve hot.

SPINACH AND FETA-STUFFED PORTOBELLOS

These are delicious all by themselves, but they would also make a great vegetarian burger, with the stuffed mushroom caps nestled inside crusty rolls. You could even finish these mushrooms on the grill, instead of in the oven. Just make sure to use a wide spatula to transfer them back and forth, so you don't lose any of the stuffing to the coals.

HERE'S WHAT YOU NEED

- 4 large portobello mushroom caps (about 4 inches, or 10 cm wide)
- 3 tablespoons (45 ml) olive oil, plus more for brushing
- 1 medium yellow onion, chopped (about ¾ cup, or 120 g)
- 3 scallions, chopped
- 5 ounces (140 g) baby spinach
- 1 cup (150 g) crumbled feta cheese
- ¼ cup (15 g) chopped fresh parsley
- 2 tablespoons (8 g) chopped fresh dill
- ½ teaspoon salt
- ¼ teaspoon ground black pepper

HERE'S WHAT YOU GET

4 GIANT STUFFED MUSHROOMS

HERE'S WHAT YOU DO

1. Preheat the oven to 400°F (200°C, or gas mark 6). Trim the mushroom caps: Cut off the stems and using a spoon, gently scrape off the brown gills. Chop the stems and gills together and set aside.

2. Brush the mushroom caps with a bit of olive oil, arrange on a rimmed sheet pan, and bake in the oven, gill-sides up, for 10 minutes. After 10 minutes, drain any liquids from the sheet pan and set it with the mushroom caps aside.

4. Add the scallions and spinach and cook until the spinach is wilted and any liquids in the skillet have cooked away. Transfer the mixture to a bowl and let cool for 10 minutes.

3. In the meantime, heat the 3 tablespoons (45 ml) of oil in a large skillet. Add the onion and reserved chopped mushroom stems and gills. Cook over medium heat until they are softened, about 5 minutes.

5. Add the feta cheese, parsley, dill, salt, and pepper to the bowl, mixing well.

6. Transfer the stuffing mixture into the mushroom caps, patting it evenly on the undersides, and bake for 20 minutes until the feta gets soft but the mushrooms still hold their shapes. Serve warm.

ROASTED SWEET POTATOES WITH EASY AIOLI

You will find these crispy wedges to be surprisingly addictive. If you really like a spicy kick, use hot paprika (start with 1 teaspoon instead of 2) or substitute ground chipotle chile powder for the paprika. Chipotle's spicy smokiness is dynamite in combination with the sweetness of the sweet potatoes.

HERE'S WHAT YOU NEED

ROASTED SWEET POTATOES:

2 medium sweet potatoes, peeled and cut into ¼-inch (6 mm) wedges

3 tablespoons (45 ml) olive oil

2 teaspoons paprika

1 teaspoon garlic powder

1 teaspoon salt

1 teaspoon ground black pepper

¼ teaspoon cayenne pepper (optional)

EASY AIOLI:

½ cup (115 g) mayonnaise

2 garlic cloves, minced

1 tablespoon (15 ml) fresh lemon juice

½ teaspoon salt

HERE'S WHAT YOU GET

4 SPICY-SWEET SERVINGS

A TASTY TIP If you want to keep the roasted sweet potatoes on the mild side, leave out the cayenne and prepare a spicy aioli by adding cayenne or chipotle powder to the aioli. Then you can decide how much dipping to do.

HERE'S WHAT YOU DO

1. Preheat the oven to 400°F (200°C, or gas mark 6). Line a baking sheet with parchment paper. In a large bowl, mix the sweet potatoes with the olive oil, paprika, garlic powder, salt, black pepper, and cayenne (if desired, for an extra kick). Make sure all the wedges are coated with the oil and spices.

3. While the potatoes are baking, make the aioli: In a bowl, combine the mayonnaise, garlic, lemon juice, and salt.

4. Serve the crispy hot potatoes with the cool aioli.

2. Arrange the potato wedges on a single layer on the baking sheet and bake for 25 to 35 minutes, turning the potatoes over halfway through the baking time. The potatoes are ready when they are golden, tender on the inside, and crispy on the outside.

SAUTÉED GREEN BEANS, MEDITERRANEAN STYLE

I'm picturing these green beans served on a sun-shiny patio or deck, along with some grilled herb-rubbed shrimp skewers or even some grilled sword-fish steaks with lemon juice squeezed over them. If we can't actually be in the Mediterranean, we can at least pretend, right?

HERE'S WHAT YOU NEED

1 pound (455 g) green beans
3 tablespoons (45 ml) olive oil, plus more for drizzling
4 garlic cloves, minced
1 large tomato, diced
Zest and juice of 1 lemon
1 cup (150 g) crumbled feta cheese
¼ cup (35 g) sliced pitted Kalamata olives
Salt and ground black pepper to taste
2 tablespoons (8 g) chopped fresh parsley
2 tablespoons (5 g) chopped fresh basil

HERE'S WHAT YOU GET

4 AL FRESCO–WORTHY SERVINGS

A TASTY TIP Regular green beans work great in this recipe, but if you see the thin haricots verts in your supermarket, give those a try instead. Because they cook quickly, you'll only need to blanch them for a minute or two in the first step.

HERE'S WHAT YOU DO

1. Bring a large pot of water to a boil. Drop the green beans into the water and blanch for 6 minutes. Drain the beans in a colander under cold running water to stop the cooking.

3. Add the tomato and the lemon zest and juice and sauté until the tomato softens, 3 to 4 minutes.

2. Heat the olive oil in a large skillet over medium heat. Add the green beans and cook for 3 minutes and then add the garlic and sauté for 1 minute more.

4. Add the feta cheese and olives to the skillet and stir to warm them up (don't cook for so long that the feta melts). Season with salt and pepper to taste.

5. Transfer the beans to a serving dish. Sprinkle with the parsley and basil and drizzle some olive oil over the top, if you like. Serve warm.

OVEN-ROASTED RATATOUILLE

Roasting is such an easy way to cook vegetables. It preserves all their nutrition and enhances their natural sweetness as well. In this recipe, you can just pile them all together onto the same baking sheet, too, making matters even more convenient. Serve this as a side dish to a protein like chicken breast or slice up a crusty baguette next to a big bowl of this ratatouille and call it a meal.

HERE'S WHAT YOU NEED

4 large tomatoes (1 pound, or 455 g), cut into 1-inch (2.5 cm) pieces

2 medium red onions, diced

2 medium zucchini (1 pound, or 455 g), cut into 1-inch (2.5 cm) pieces

1 medium eggplant (1 pound, or 455 g) cut into 1-inch (2.5 cm) pieces

1 large yellow or red bell pepper, cut in half, seeded, each half cut into ¼-inch (6 mm) strips

4 garlic cloves, minced

1 tablespoon (3 g) herbes de Provence

2 teaspoons salt, plus more as needed

1 teaspoon ground black pepper, plus more as needed

¼ cup (60 ml) olive oil

¼ cup (10 g) chopped fresh basil

HERE'S WHAT YOU GET

4 TO 6 FLAVORFUL SERVINGS

A TASTY TIP You can serve a delicious cold version of this ratatouille the next day by stirring in some capers, chopped black or green olives, and wine vinegar. Drizzle it all with some more olive oil.

HERE'S WHAT YOU DO

1. Preheat the oven to 400°F (200°C, or gas mark 6). In a large bowl, mix the tomatoes, onions, zucchini, eggplant, bell pepper, garlic, herbes de Provence, salt, pepper, and olive oil.

3. Transfer the vegetables to a large baking sheet and roast in the oven for 30 to 40 minutes, turning the vegetables occasionally to make sure they cook evenly.

4. Transfer the vegetables to a serving dish. Taste and season with more salt and pepper, if desired. Sprinkle with the fresh basil. The ratatouille can be served warm or at room temperature.

2. Stir well to make sure all of the vegetables are nicely coated with the oil and spices.

ZUCCHINI PANCAKES

Pancakes make vegetables a lot more fun, right? You feel virtuous because you are eating your veggies, but you also feel like you're indulging in something—because they're pancakes. These savory cakes are as tasty at breakfast as they are at dinnertime.

HERE'S WHAT YOU NEED

2 cups grated zucchini (1½ to 2 small zucchini)

2 large eggs, lightly beaten

¼ cup (25 g) grated Parmesan, pecorino, or Romano cheese

3 tablespoons (30 g) grated yellow onion

2 tablespoons (8 g) chopped fresh parsley

2 tablespoons (5 g) chopped fresh basil

½ cup (63 g) all-purpose flour

½ teaspoon baking powder

½ teaspoon salt

¼ teaspoon ground black pepper

Vegetable oil, for cooking

HERE'S WHAT YOU GET

8 VEGGIE-FILLED PANCAKES

HERE'S WHAT YOU DO

1. Preheat the oven to 200°F (93°C) and set a baking sheet in the oven. Dry the grated zucchini in a clean kitchen towel by making a bundle and twisting the top to release as much liquid as possible. Dry zucchini will make for light, crispy pancakes (but wet zucchini will make for heavy, soggy pancakes, so beware).

2. Transfer the zucchini to a large bowl and add the eggs, cheese, onion, parsley, and basil, mixing well to combine everything evenly.

3. In a small bowl, mix the flour, baking powder, salt, and pepper. Add the flour mixture to the zucchini mixture, combining everything into a thick batter.

4. Heat 2 tablespoons (28 ml) of the vegetable oil in a large skillet over medium heat. Drop large tablespoonfuls (15 g) of the zucchini batter into the hot oil, flattening them slightly so their thickness is even. Cook until golden, 2 to 3 minutes per side.

5. As you finish cooking the pancakes, transfer them to the baking sheet in the warm oven. Continue until all the pancakes are cooked. Serve right away.

BREADCRUMB-TOPPED STUFFED TOMATOES

This is a great dish to make in the summertime, when you can get big, juicy beefsteak or heirloom tomatoes. They make a pretty, elegant side dish for practically anything coming off the grill. Plus, they're just as tasty served at room temperature as they are served hot.

HERE'S WHAT YOU NEED

4 large tomatoes
2 tablespoons (28 ml) olive oil, plus more for drizzling
1 small yellow onion, diced (1 cup, or 160 g)
2 garlic cloves, minced
1 teaspoon salt
½ teaspoon ground black pepper
¼ teaspoon red pepper flakes (optional)
1 cup (100 g) finely grated pecorino or Parmesan cheese, divided
1 tablespoon (7 g) breadcrumbs
2 tablespoons (5 g) chopped fresh basil

HERE'S WHAT YOU GET

4 SOFT AND LUSCIOUS STUFFED TOMATOES

HERE'S WHAT YOU DO

1. Preheat the oven to 350°F (180°C, or gas mark 4). Slice off the top one-quarter of each tomato and set aside. With a small spoon or a melon baller, clean out the inside of the tomatoes, saving the "tomato meat" and chopping it along with the tomato tops. Set the chopped-up tomato parts aside.

A TASTY TIP Choose tomatoes that are ripe but firm. Firm "shells" will hold up better in the oven.

2. Heat the olive oil in a large nonstick skillet over medium heat. Add the onion and cook until softened, about 5 minutes.

3. Add the garlic, reserved chopped tomato parts, salt, black pepper, and red pepper flakes, if desired. Cook until the mixture is thickened, 10 to 15 minutes.

4. Take the skillet off the heat and stir in ½ cup (50 g) of the cheese.

5. Using a spoon and being careful not to tear the tomato cups, transfer the filling mixture into the tomato cups.

6. Place the stuffed tomatoes on a baking sheet and top each evenly with the breadcrumbs and the remaining ½ cup (50 g) of the cheese. Bake for 10 to 15 minutes until the tomatoes get soft (but not too soft—you don't want them to fall apart).

7. Transfer the tomatoes to a plate or platter. Drizzle with any accumulated juice from the baking sheet, sprinkle with the chopped basil, and add a final drizzle of olive oil.

BRUSSELS SPROUTS WITH BACON and PARMESAN

Brussels sprouts had a poor reputation for a long time, being treated so badly by being boiled to within an inch of their life. Now they are getting all kinds of star treatment with proper cooking methods and the addition of premium ingredients. Here, the Parmesan and bacon add salty, smoky, intense flavor to these adorable mini cabbages.

HERE'S WHAT YOU NEED

1 pound (455 g) brussels sprouts, ends trimmed and cut in half
8 ounces (225 g) thick-sliced bacon, diced
1 cup (160 g) diced yellow or red onion
Freshly cracked black pepper to taste
1 cup (100 g) grated Parmesan cheese

HERE'S WHAT YOU GET

4 FLAVOR-PACKED SERVINGS OF HEALTHY BRASSICAS

HERE'S WHAT YOU DO

1. Preheat the oven to 350°F (180°C, or gas mark 4). Bring a large pot of water to a boil. Add the brussels sprouts and cook for 5 to 8 minutes until fork-tender but not falling apart. Drain in a colander and set aside.

2. In a large skillet over medium heat, sauté the bacon until brown and crispy. Using a slotted spoon, transfer the bacon to a paper towel-lined plate to drain. Leave the fat in the skillet.

4. Add the brussels sprouts and sauté until browned on all sides, about 10 minutes.

3. In the same skillet, in the bacon fat, sauté the onion until softened, about 5 minutes.

5. Transfer everything to a 9 x 13-inch (23 x 33 cm) baking dish, fold in the cooked bacon, season with a twist or two of cracked pepper, and then shower everything with the Parmesan.

6. Bake in the oven for 10 to 15 minutes until the cheese is golden and crispy. Serve hot.

MEXICAN-STYLE CORN ON THE COB

Called *elote*, this is a traditional Mexican street food. Food carts there grill the corn, but you can certainly boil or steam it instead if that's your preferred method of cooking corn on the cob. You could also try using sour cream instead of the mayonnaise and ancho chile powder in place of the cayenne.

HERE'S WHAT YOU NEED

¼ cup (60 g) mayonnaise
1 tablespoon (15 g) sour cream
1 teaspoon grated lime zest
1 tablespoon (15 ml) fresh lime juice
1 large garlic clove, minced
4 to 6 ears corn on the cob
Salt (optional)
½ cup (75 g) crumbled Cotija or feta cheese
Cayenne pepper to taste
¼ cup (4 g) chopped fresh cilantro
Lime wedges, for serving

HERE'S WHAT YOU GET

4 TO 6 SLATHERED EARS OF CORN

A TASTY TIP When shucking the corn, don't break off the end stalks of the corncobs. These will serve as a useful "handle" for eating the corn, which will be kind of slippery from all the saucy, cheesy goodness.

HERE'S WHAT YOU DO

1. In a bowl, mix the mayonnaise, sour cream, lime zest and juice, and garlic to make a smooth sauce.

2. Cook the corn to your preference. To boil, bring a large pot of salted water to a boil and boil the corn for about 5 minutes. To steam, set up a large pot with a steamer basket and steam the corn over boiling water for about 10 minutes. To grill, either put the corn directly on the grill or wrap it in aluminum foil and grill for about 15 minutes, turning it a few times during grilling.

3. When the corn is ready and it is still hot, lay the cobs on a large platter and brush them all over with the sauce mixture.

4. Sprinkle the cobs with the cheese (pressing it lightly into the sauce to make it stick), sprinkle the cheese with your preferred amount of cayenne, and then sprinkle the cilantro over everything. Serve with lime wedges for squeezing.

MEAT, POULTRY, AND FISH FOR DINNER

PANKO BAKED CHICKEN CUTLETS

These crispy chicken cutlets could not be simpler or more delicious. You might not think of them as comfort food, but that's exactly what they are. And if you have leftovers (and that's a big "if"), you can slice them up cold the next day and toss them into your Caesar salad.

HERE'S WHAT YOU NEED

Nonstick cooking spray
4 boneless, skinless chicken breasts
3 tablespoons (45 g) Dijon mustard, plus more for serving
1 cup (112 g) panko
1 cup (100 g) grated Parmesan cheese
1 teaspoon ground black pepper

HERE'S WHAT YOU GET

8 CRISPY, JUICY CUTLETS

HERE'S WHAT YOU DO

1. Preheat the oven to 425°F (220°C, or gas mark 7). Line a baking sheet with parchment paper and spray with nonstick cooking spray. Cut each chicken breast in half horizontally so you end up with 8 thin cutlets.

Variation

For an easy version of chicken parm, lay the cooked chicken in a 9 x 13-inch (23 x 33 cm) baking dish instead of on the baking sheet. Pour tomato sauce over the tops of the cutlets, sprinkle shredded mozzarella on top, and bake for 15 minutes until the chicken is heated through, the sauce is bubbling, and the cheese is melted. Serve as is or with pasta on the side.

2. Toss the cutlets in a bowl with the mustard, making sure all sides of the chicken are well coated with the mustard.

4. Lay each cutlet on the prepared baking sheet, spray the cutlets with nonstick cooking spray, and bake in the oven for 10 to 12 minutes.

3. In a shallow plate or bowl, mix the panko, Parmesan, and pepper. Dredge each cutlet into the breading mixture, making sure all sides of the chicken are well coated with the mixture.

5. Take the baking sheet out of the oven. Using tongs, turn the cutlets over, spray the other side with nonstick cooking spray, and bake for 10 to 12 minutes more until golden and crispy.

6. Serve hot, with more Dijon mustard on the side for dipping, if you like.

NOT-QUITE KITCHEN-SINK STIR-FRY

It may look like a long list of ingredients here, but don't be put off. Just have everything all assembled and ready because the actual cooking will go super-fast once you get started. Serve this over cooked rice or Asian noodles.

HERE'S WHAT YOU NEED

½ cup (120 ml) chicken broth
3 tablespoons (45 ml) soy sauce
2 tablespoons (28 ml) rice vinegar
2 tablespoons (28 g) light brown sugar
3 tablespoons (45 ml) toasted sesame oil
1 tablespoon (8 g) grated fresh ginger
2 garlic cloves, minced
½ cup (70 g) sliced shiitake mushrooms
5 scallions, cut into 2-inch (5 cm) pieces, plus more, chopped, for garnish
1 large carrot, peeled and thinly sliced , blanched
1 cup (110 g) green beans, cut into 1-inch (2.5 cm) pieces, blanched
4 baby bok choy, quartered
8 to 10 ounces (225 to 280 g) leftover cooked chicken, cut into bite-size pieces
Fresh cilantro, for garnish (optional)

HERE'S WHAT YOU GET

2 SAUCY STIR-FRIED SERVINGS

HERE'S WHAT YOU DO

1. In a bowl, mix the chicken broth, soy sauce, rice vinegar, and brown sugar. Set aside.

2. Heat the sesame oil in a wok or large skillet over high heat. Add the ginger and garlic and cook, stirring quickly, until fragrant, about 1 minute. Add the mushrooms and cook until starting to get soft, about 3 minutes.

4. Add the bok choy and continue cooking and stirring until the boy choy is wilted and bright in color.

3. Add the scallions, carrots, and green beans and cook until the vegetables are bright in color and the scallions are wilted, about 4 to 5 minutes.

5. Add the reserved chicken broth mixture and the chicken and let everything come to a boil for a few minutes until the sauce thickens.

6. Serve immediately, garnished with the scallions and cilantro, if you like.

JUICIEST TURKEY BURGERS

Turkey burgers often get a bad rap, resulting from one too many dried-out sorry substitutes for a regular beef burger in a pub or restaurant. This recipe should help restore their reputation. Look for ground turkey that's a mix of light and dark meat. For the juiciest burgers, in general, "extra-lean" is a phrase you want to avoid.

HERE'S WHAT YOU NEED

1 pound (455 g) ground turkey
¼ cup (40 g) minced red onion
3 tablespoons (19 g) finely chopped Kalamata olives
1 teaspoon dried oregano
½ teaspoon ground cumin
½ teaspoon salt
½ teaspoon ground black pepper
2 tablespoons (28 ml) olive oil
4 burger buns
Your favorite condiments, for serving

HERE'S WHAT YOU GET

4 TENDER TURKEY BURGERS

A TASTY TIP For a change of pace, serve tucked into pita breads (or buns) with thinly sliced cucumbers and tomatoes and a bit of feta cheese. Or serve on brioche rolls with lettuce and honey mustard.

HERE'S WHAT YOU DO

1. In a large bowl, mix the turkey, onion, olives, oregano, cumin, salt, and pepper, making sure all the ingredients get evenly distributed. Really, the best way to do this is with your clean hands. Be careful not to overmix or your burgers will turn out dense and tough. And don't forget to wash your hands thoroughly after mixing the meat.

3. Heat the olive oil in a very large skillet over medium-high heat (or divide it between 2 medium skillets). Add the burgers and cook for 4 to 5 minutes on each side until cooked through and golden brown on both sides.

4. Serve the turkey patties on burger buns with your condiments of choice.

2. Divide the mixture into 4 equal-size patties.

EASY FREEFORM MEATLOAF

A lot of meatloaf recipes call for a fancy mix of different ground meats. This is a classic, tried-and-true pure ground beef version, lightened up with some vegetables as well as with the usual eggs and breadcrumbs. And it's topped with bacon! Leftovers make fantastic sandwiches, on any kind of bread you like.

HERE'S WHAT YOU NEED

2 tablespoons (28 ml) olive oil
2 carrots, peeled and diced
2 celery stalks, diced
1 medium yellow onion, diced
2 pounds (900 g) ground beef
2 large eggs, lightly beaten
1 cup (115 g) breadcrumbs
1 teaspoon dried thyme
1 teaspoon salt
½ teaspoon ground black pepper
4 tablespoons (60 g) ketchup, divided,
   plus more for serving (optional)
2 teaspoons Dijon mustard
4 slices of bacon

HERE'S WHAT YOU GET

1 JUICY MEATLOAF TO SERVE ABOUT 8 PEOPLE

HERE'S WHAT YOU DO

1. Preheat the oven to 350°F (180°C, or gas mark 4). Line a baking sheet with parchment paper. Heat the olive oil in a large skillet over medium heat. Sauté the carrots, celery, and onion until softened, about 8 minutes. Set aside to cool.

2. In a large bowl, mix the ground beef with the cooled cooked vegetables.

3. Add the eggs, breadcrumbs, thyme, salt, pepper, 1 tablespoon (15 g) of the ketchup, and the mustard. Mix well to combine evenly, but be careful not to overmix or your meatloaf will be tough. The best way to mix this is with your clean hands.

4. Transfer the meatloaf mixture to the prepared baking sheet and shape it into a roughly 5 x 9-inch (13 x 23 cm) loaf shape.

5. Brush the loaf with the remaining 3 tablespoons (45 ml) of ketchup and cover it with the bacon slices.

6. Bake for about 1 hour until the bacon is crispy and the juices are running clear from the meatloaf when you pierce it through the middle. If you have an instant-read thermometer, it should read 160°F (71°C) when inserted into the middle of the meatloaf.

7. Serve hot, with more ketchup on the side, if you like.

ITALIAN MEATBALLS

Here's an Italian-American grandmother pro tip: Slice open a crusty deli roll, spread it with softened salted butter, and then take a couple of these crusty-on-the-outside, tender-on-the-inside meatballs and mash them coarsely into the buttered roll. You'll never look back.

HERE'S WHAT YOU NEED

¾ cup (90 g) dried breadcrumbs
½ cup (120 ml) milk
1¾ pounds (795 g) ground beef
8 ounces (225 g) ground pork
1 medium yellow onion, minced
3 garlic cloves, minced
½ cup (30 g) minced fresh parsley
2 large eggs, lightly beaten
1 cup (100 g) grated Parmesan cheese
1 teaspoon salt
1 teaspoon ground black pepper
½ cup (63 g) all-purpose flour
Olive oil, for cooking

HERE'S WHAT YOU GET

30 NANA-WORTHY MEATBALLS

A TASTY TIP Instead of finishing the meatballs in the oven, add them to your favorite tomato sauce after you brown them and simmer for 30 to 45 minutes to finish cooking them through. Serve with Italian bread or pasta.

HERE'S WHAT YOU DO

1. Preheat the oven to 350°F (180°C, or gas mark 4). In a small bowl, mix the breadcrumbs and milk. Let sit for 10 minutes so the crumbs can soak up the milk.

3. Put the flour in a shallow plate. Shape the meatballs into 2-inch (5 cm) balls and roll them in the flour.

2. In a large bowl, mix the beef, pork, breadcrumb-milk mixture, onion, garlic, parsley, eggs, Parmesan, salt, and pepper, making sure all the ingredients are evenly distributed without overmixing them. You want your meatballs to be light and fluffy, not like golf balls. The best way to mix these ingredients is with your clean hands.

4. Heat 2 to 3 tablespoons (28 to 45 ml) of olive oil in a large skillet over medium heat. Brown the meatballs on all sides (you are not cooking them all the way through at this point—although you could if you wanted). You will need to brown the meatballs in a few batches, so add more oil to the skillet as needed. Drain the meatballs on paper towels.

5. Arrange the browned meatballs on a baking sheet and transfer them to the oven to finish cooking, 30 to 45 minutes. Serve warm.

CLASSIC ROAST CHICKEN

A whole roast chicken is a really impressive company meal. Plus, it's easy and economical. It takes a little while in the oven, but it's mostly hands-off time, leaving you free to mix cocktails or pour more wine.

HERE'S WHAT YOU NEED

1 whole chicken (3½ to 4 pounds, or 1.6 to 1.8 kg), left at room temperature for 20 minutes
Salt and ground black pepper to taste
1 lemon, cut in half
5 sprigs of fresh thyme
5 sprigs of fresh parsley
4 garlic cloves, minced
2 tablespoons (28 g) unsalted butter, softened
2 medium carrots, peeled and cut into 2-inch (5 cm) chunks
1 yellow onion, cut in half and each half quartered

HERE'S WHAT YOU GET

1 BEAUTIFUL ROAST CHICKEN TO SERVE 4 OR 5

A TASTY TIP If so inclined, put the roasting pan on the top of the stove over medium-high heat. Add 1 tablespoon (14 g) of butter. When it melts, add ½ cup (120 ml) of chicken broth, scraping the bottom of the pan to scrape up any tasty browned bits. Bring it to a boil for a few minutes until thickened. Serve this pan gravy with the chicken.

HERE'S WHAT YOU DO

1. Preheat the oven to 400°F (200°C, or gas mark 6). Remove the giblets from the chicken cavity, if they are there. Discard or save for another use. Prepare the chicken by generously sprinkling the inside with salt and pepper.

2. Squeeze one half of the lemon into the cavity and the other half over the chicken. Stuff the cavity with the thyme and parsley sprigs and the squeezed lemon halves.

3. Mix the garlic and butter together and, opening the breast skin very carefully, insert all the butter over the breast, spreading it between the meat and skin and trying not to tear the skin.

4. Tie the legs together with kitchen string and put the chicken in a large cast iron pan or roasting pan. Sprinkle it generously with salt and pepper and scatter the carrots and onion all around the chicken.

5. Roast for 1 to 1½ hours, basting the chicken a few times with the juices that accumulate in the bottom of the pan. Let rest for 10 minutes before carving the chicken. Serve it with the roasted vegetables.

FLAKY CHICKEN POTPIE

With its brothy gravy and its golden top crust, bursting with chicken and veggies, chicken potpie is serious comfort food. This recipe uses puff pastry for a lighter, flakier top crust, but you could use traditional pie dough instead if you prefer. Leftovers keep well in the fridge and can be quickly micro-waved for lunch later in the week.

HERE'S WHAT YOU NEED

6 tablespoons (85 g) unsalted butter, plus more for preparing the baking dish
6 tablespoons (95 g) all-purpose flour
2 cups (475 ml) chicken broth
1 cup (235 ml) milk, plus more if needed
2 tablespoons (28 ml) olive oil
1 medium yellow onion, diced
1 cup (130 g) diced carrot
1 cup (120 g) diced celery
½ teaspoon salt
½ teaspoon ground black pepper
4 cups (560 g) chopped cooked chicken
1 cup (130 g) frozen peas
1 sheet frozen puff pastry, thawed, rolled with a rolling pin to 8 x 11-inch (20 x 28 cm) size, if necessary

HERE'S WHAT YOU GET

4 TO 6 HOMEY, COMFORTING SERVINGS

HERE'S WHAT YOU DO

1. Preheat the oven to 375°F (190°C, or gas mark 5). Butter an 8 x 11-inch (20 x 28 cm) baking dish. In a large saucepan over medium heat, melt the 6 tablespoons (85 g) of butter. Add the flour while whisking and cook for about a minute.

2. Slowly add the chicken broth, whisking until it's slightly thickened. Add the milk and cook, without letting it come to a boil, until the mixture has thickened a bit more, about 5 minutes. Remove from the heat and set aside.

4. Add the sautéed vegetables, the chicken, and the frozen peas to the saucepan with the sauce, mixing everything to get the sauce to coat all the ingredients. If it seems too dry, add a bit more milk.

3. Heat the olive oil in a large skillet over medium-high heat and sauté the onion, carrots, and celery until softened, about 6 minutes. Season with the salt and pepper.

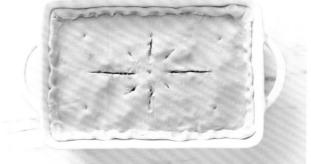

5. Transfer the entire mixture into the buttered baking dish. Carefully drape the puff pastry sheet over the casserole and poke a few holes here and there, as you would for a pie.

6. Bake for 45 minutes or until the puff pastry is puffy and golden and the inside is bubbling through the holes in the top of the pastry. Serve hot.

GAME DAY SAUSAGE AND PEPPERS

Use sweet or hot Italian sausages in this dish, as you like. You could use all one kind of bell pepper, but your finished dish will be less colorful that way (and why would you want that?). In the wintertime, serve this with rice or pasta. In the summertime, stuff the sausages and peppers into sub rolls and turn on the baseball game.

HERE'S WHAT YOU NEED

1 red bell pepper
1 yellow bell pepper
1 green bell pepper
2 large yellow onions
1 tablespoon (15 ml) olive oil
2 pounds (900 g) sweet or hot Italian sausage links
½ teaspoon salt
½ teaspoon ground black pepper
1 cup (180 g) chopped tomato

HERE'S WHAT YOU GET

6 REGULAR SERVINGS OR
4 BALLPARK SERVINGS

HERE'S WHAT YOU DO

1. Cut the bell peppers into slices ¼-inch (6 mm) thick.

2. Peel the onions, cut the onions in half, and then cut each half into slices ¼-inch (6 mm) thick slices.

4. Add the bell peppers to the oil left in the pan and cook on medium heat for 2 minutes. Add the onions and cook until the peppers and onions are soft and lightly browned, about 10 minutes. Season with the salt and pepper.

3. Heat the olive oil in a large skillet over medium heat. Brown the sausages on all sides in the hot oil. Transfer the sausages to a plate, leaving the oil in the pan.

5. Return the sausages to the skillet, add the chopped tomato, and cook for about 20 minutes until the sausages are cooked through and the onions and peppers are meltingly soft.

6. Serve hot.

SIMPLIFIED CHICKEN LEGS a L'ORANGE

Traditionally, this preparation was made with duck and involved many more ingredients, including wine or orange liqueur, duck stock, and so forth. This is a far simpler but nonetheless delicious version. There is also some debate about whether the dish originated in France or Italy. No matter: It was our own American Julia Child who actually brought it to popular acclaim.

HERE'S WHAT YOU NEED

1 cup (125 g) all-purpose flour
1 teaspoon garlic powder
1 teaspoon salt
½ teaspoon ground black pepper
4 whole chicken legs
2 tablespoons (28 ml) olive oil
2 tablespoons (28 g) unsalted butter
1 cup (235 ml) orange juice

HERE'S WHAT YOU GET

4 ACHIEVABLE SERVINGS

HERE'S WHAT YOU DO

1. Preheat the oven to 375°F (190°C, or gas mark 5). In a large resealable plastic bag, mix the flour, garlic powder, salt, and pepper. One at a time, drop the chicken legs into the bag and shake until they are evenly coated with the flour mixture. Set the chicken legs on a plate.

2. Heat the olive oil over medium-high heat in a cast iron skillet large enough to accommodate the chicken legs. Add the chicken legs, skin-side up, and brown for about 3 minutes. Then turn and brown the other side.

3. Cover the skillet loosely with aluminum foil and transfer it to the oven. Bake for 30 minutes and then remove the aluminum foil and turn the legs over. Return the skillet to the oven, uncovered, and bake for 15 to 20 minutes more.

4. Transfer the chicken legs to a serving platter. Carefully transfer the skillet to the stovetop and, holding the handle with an oven mitt, melt the butter in the skillet over medium-high heat. Add the orange juice and bring to a boil, scraping the bottom of the pan with a wooden spoon to bring all the ingredients together. Let the sauce thicken a bit.

5. Pour the sauce over the chicken legs or serve on the side.

BEEF AND MULTI-BEAN CHILI

Chili is pretty forgiving, so you can easily adjust the ingredients to suit your mood. Use hot chili powder and more jalapeños to make a rip-your-lips-off chili. Use only one kind of bean—or add pinto beans right along with the kidney and black beans. Use fewer tomatoes to make it less tomato-ey. And then there are the garnishes (see the Tasty Tip)—the possibilities seem endless.

HERE'S WHAT YOU NEED

3 tablespoons (45 ml) olive oil
1 red bell pepper, diced
1 or 2 jalapeños, minced (optional)
1 medium red onion, diced
3 garlic cloves, minced
2 pounds (900 g) ground beef
2 tablespoons (14 g) ground cumin
1 to 2 tablespoons (8 to 15 g) chili powder (as desired)
1 tablespoon (3 g) dried oregano
2 teaspoons salt
1 teaspoon ground black pepper
1 can (14 ounces, or 390 g) of diced tomatoes
1 cup (245 g) tomato sauce
1 can (15 ounces) of red kidney beans, rinsed and drained
1 can (15 ounces) of black beans, rinsed and drained

HERE'S WHAT YOU GET

6 TO 8 BEEFY, BEANY SERVINGS

A TASTY TIP Dress this up for serving with any—or all—of the following: shredded Cheddar cheese, chopped avocado, sliced radishes, pickled jalapeños, chopped red onion, chopped fresh cilantro, sliced scallions, salsa, and/or sour cream.

HERE'S WHAT YOU DO

1. Heat the olive oil in a Dutch oven over medium heat. Add the bell pepper, jalapeño (if desired), onion, and garlic and cook until the vegetables are softened, about 5 minutes.

3. Add the cumin, chili powder, oregano, salt, and pepper and mix everything together well.

2. Add the ground beef, breaking it up with a wooden spoon and cooking until it is no longer pink, 6 to 8 minutes.

4. Add the tomatoes and tomato sauce. Reduce the heat to a simmer, cover, and cook for 20 to 30 minutes.

5. Uncover, add the kidney beans and black beans, and simmer for 15 minutes more. Taste the chili and adjust the seasoning as desired. Serve hot, with any desired garnishes.

TRUE SHEPHERD'S PIE

Shepherd's pie is a meaty, savory comfort food classic. It's defined by the fact that it has mashed potatoes for a top crust rather than pastry. And ground lamb is the traditional meat for a shepherd's pie, but other than that, the dish can vary greatly in its ingredients. (If you want to make it with ground beef instead, please call it cottage pie.) Make this on a weekend and then devour it all week long.

HERE'S WHAT YOU NEED

1½ pounds (680 g) Yukon Gold potatoes, cut into cubes, cooked, and kept hot

2 tablespoons (28 g) unsalted butter

2 tablespoons (28 g) sour cream

2 teaspoons salt, divided

1 teaspoon ground black pepper, divided

¾ cup (90 g) shredded Cheddar cheese, divided

2 tablespoons (28 ml) olive oil

1 cup (160 g) chopped yellow or white onion

1 large carrot, peeled and diced

3 garlic cloves, minced

2 pounds (900 g) ground lamb

1 medium tomato, chopped

1 tablespoon (15 g) ketchup

½ cup (120 ml) beef broth

½ cup (82 g) frozen corn kernels

½ cup (65 g) frozen peas

HERE'S WHAT YOU GET

6 HOT AND HEARTY SERVINGS

HERE'S WHAT YOU DO

1. Preheat the oven to 400°F (200°C, or gas mark 6). In a large bowl, mash or blend the hot potatoes with the butter, sour cream, 1 teaspoon salt, ½ teaspoon of pepper, and ½ cup (58 g) of the Cheddar cheese. Set aside.

2. Heat the olive oil in a large skillet over medium-high heat. Sauté the onion, carrot, and garlic until softened, about 6 minutes.

3. Add the lamb, remaining teaspoon of salt, and ½ teaspoon of pepper. Cook, breaking up the lamb with a wooden spoon, for about 15 minutes until the lamb is no longer pink. Put a colander in the sink and drain the lamb mixture to get rid of all the accumulated fat in the skillet.

4. Return the lamb mixture to the skillet and add the tomato, ketchup, and broth. Bring to a boil and then add the corn and peas and stir to combine everything.

5. Transfer the mixture to an 8 x 11-inch (20 x 28 cm) baking dish. Top with the potato mixture and then sprinkle the top evenly with the remaining ¼ cup (30 g) of Cheddar cheese.

6. Bake for 30 minutes until the potatoes are golden and the filling is bubbly. Serve hot.

ROAST BEEF TENDERLOIN with HORSERADISH SAUCE

Beef tenderloin is very lean, so be careful not to overcook it since the lack of fat could cause it to dry out if it's overdone. And because its flavor is more mild and subtler than, say, a prime rib, we are amping it up with a zesty horseradish sauce. This is a simple and elegant preparation that is great if you are hosting a holiday or having a special evening at home.

HERE'S WHAT YOU NEED

TENDERLOIN:

2½ to 3 pounds (1.1 to 1.4 kg) beef tenderloin, trimmed and tied if necessary for even thickness

2 tablespoons (28 ml) olive oil

1 teaspoon salt

1 teaspoon ground black pepper

1 tablespoon (2 g) chopped fresh rosemary

2 garlic cloves, minced

HORSERADISH SAUCE:

½ cup (115 g) mayonnaise

½ cup (115 g) sour cream

½ cup (120 g) prepared horseradish, drained

¼ cup (60 g) Dijon mustard

1 teaspoon salt

1 teaspoon ground black pepper

HERE'S WHAT YOU GET

6 TO 8 SHOW-STOPPING SERVINGS

A TASTY TIP If you think the horseradish is too strong a flavor, skip it, and increase the amount of Dijon mustard to ½ cup (60 g). Stir 3 tablespoons (12 g) of chopped fresh parsley into the sauce.

HERE'S WHAT YOU DO

1. Preheat the oven to 400°F (200°C, or gas mark 6). Let the tenderloin sit at room temperature for 30 minutes. Put the tenderloin on a baking sheet or in a roasting pan. Rub it all over with the olive oil. Season with the salt, pepper, rosemary, and garlic.

3. Take the tenderloin out of the oven and let it rest, loosely covered with aluminum foil, for 10 to 15 minutes before cutting.

2. Transfer to the oven and roast for 35 to 40 minutes for medium-rare. This is a good occasion to use a meat thermometer, if you have one, to make sure you cook the meat to no higher than 140°F (60°C).

4. In the meantime, in a bowl, mix together the mayonnaise, sour cream, horseradish, mustard, salt, and pepper.

5. Slice the tenderloin into slices ¼ inch (6 mm) thick, arrange on a serving platter, and serve with the Horseradish Sauce alongside.

MOULES MARINIERES

The name of this culinary classic from Normandy, on the rugged north coast of France, translates as "mussels sailor style." Serve the mussels with chunks of crusty French baguette for soaking up all the deliciously briny pot juices. And don't forget to serve the rest of the white wine from the bottle, too.

HERE'S WHAT YOU NEED

3 tablespoons (42 g) unsalted butter
1 large yellow onion, diced
3 garlic cloves, minced
1 large or 2 small tomatoes, seeded and chopped
4 to 5 pounds (1.8 to 2.3 kg) mussels, debearded
⅔ cup (160 ml) dry white wine
5 tablespoons (20 g) chopped fresh parsley

HERE'S WHAT YOU GET

4 SAILOR-STYLE SERVINGS

HERE'S WHAT YOU DO

1. In a very large stockpot (large enough to move all the mussels around), melt the butter over medium heat. Add the onion and garlic and sauté until softened, about 5 minutes.

3. Add the cleaned mussels and stir until they are coated with the vegetables. Add the wine and cover the pot to allow the mussels to steam.

2. Add the tomatoes and stir until they are softened and release a bit of their juice, 2 to 3 minutes.

4. After 10 minutes, check the pot and give the mussels a stir, checking at the same time to see if all the mussels have opened. Put the lid back on, turn the heat off, and let sit for another 3 minutes. Discard any mussels that remain closed.

5. Toss the mussels with the parsley. You can serve the mussels right from the pot or transfer the mussels to one large serving bowl or several individual bowls. Be sure to include the cooking liquid from the pot.

SOLE MEUNIÈRE

Here's another French classic that is easy enough to make for dinner anytime. Sole is light and delicate in flavor and is well complemented by the buttery sauce. In classic French restaurant service, the whole fish is sautéed and then the cooking is finished and the fish is filleted tableside, in front of the diners. But don't worry—we're practicing modern service here.

HERE'S WHAT YOU NEED

¾ cup (94 g) all-purpose flour
1 teaspoon salt
½ teaspoon ground black pepper
8 sole fillets (or other thin white fish fillets)
½ cup (1 stick, or 112 g) unsalted butter, divided
Juice of 3 lemons
3 tablespoons (12 g) chopped fresh parsley

HERE'S WHAT YOU GET

4 BUTTERY, LEMONY SERVINGS

A TASTY TIP In the last step, you can let the butter brown a bit if you like, before adding the lemon juice. This will add a wonderfully nutty flavor to the sauce.

HERE'S WHAT YOU DO

1. Stir together the flour, salt, and pepper in a shallow plate. Dredge the fillets in the seasoned flour, making sure to coat all sides.

3. Transfer to a platter, cover to keep warm, and repeat with 2 more tablespoons (28 g) of the butter and the remaining 4 fillets. Transfer these fillets to the platter with the first batch.

2. In a large skillet, melt 2 tablespoons (28 g) of the butter over medium-high heat. Place 4 fillets in the melted butter and lower the heat to medium. Cook the fillets for 2 minutes on each side.

4. Melt the remaining 4 tablespoons (55 g) of butter in the skillet. Add the lemon juice and cook, letting it bubble and thicken slightly.

5. Pour the sauce over the sole. Sprinkle with the parsley and serve right away.

EASY CLAM CHOWDER

With the ready availability of good-quality canned chopped clams, this chowder is a snap to put together. Good-quality clam juice is readily available, too; look for it near the canned clams in the tuna aisle of your supermarket. One spoonful of this chowder will transport you to the wild, rocky coast of New England.

HERE'S WHAT YOU NEED

1 teaspoon vegetable oil
2 thick slices of bacon, diced
1 white onion, diced (about 1 cup, or 160 g)
1 large or 2 small Yukon Gold potatoes, diced
2 cups (475 ml) clam juice or vegetable broth
2 cups (224 g) chopped clams, undrained
1½ cups (355 ml) heavy cream
Oyster crackers, for serving

HERE'S WHAT YOU GET

4 TO 6 SEASIDE-WORTHY SERVINGS

HERE'S WHAT YOU DO

1. In a large pot, heat the vegetable oil over medium heat and sauté the bacon until soft but not crisp, 2 to 3 minutes. Add the onion and sauté until translucent, 5 to 7 minutes.

A TASTY TIP If you like a good corn chowder, you could add a small can of sweet corn kernels, drained, when you add the clams.

2. Add the potatoes to the pot, stirring to coat them with the onions and the bacon.

4. Add the clams and their juices and simmer for 2 minutes.

3. Add the clam juice or broth and bring to a boil and then reduce the heat and simmer until the potatoes are starting to get soft, about 5 minutes.

5. Add the heavy cream and let the chowder get hot, stirring occasionally, without letting it come to a boil.

6. Serve the chowder with oyster crackers.

BAKED SALMON EN PAPILLOTTE

En papillotte means to bake something in parchment paper, but it's much easier to work with aluminum foil to create an airtight packet, so that's what you'll do here. The salmon steams in the oven inside the foil packet, keeping it incredibly moist and delicate in texture. This technique also allows you to cut way down on the fat needed for cooking. And it makes for a spectacular presentation when the foil is opened.

HERE'S WHAT YOU NEED

1 pound (455 g) skin-on salmon fillet
Salt and ground black pepper to taste
1 large scallion, thinly sliced
3 tablespoons (12 g) chopped fresh dill, divided
4 thin slices of lemon
½ cup (120 ml) chicken broth or dry white wine
1 cup (230 g) sour cream
3 tablespoons (45 g) whole-grain mustard
1 tablespoon (15 ml) fresh lemon juice

HERE'S WHAT YOU GET

2 TO 4 MOIST AND DELICIOUS SERVINGS

Variation

This method of cooking in a foil packet works brilliantly for most types of fish fillets, like cod, halibut, trout, and bass.

HERE'S WHAT YOU DO

1. Preheat the oven to 400°F (200°C, or gas mark 6). Cut a large piece of heavy-duty aluminum foil twice the length of the salmon and place it on a baking sheet. Place the salmon on the foil. Sprinkle with salt and pepper, the scallions, and 2 tablespoons (8 g) of the dill. Lay the lemon slices on top.

3. In the meantime, in a bowl, mix together the sour cream, mustard, and lemon juice. Season with salt and pepper to taste.

4. When the fish is ready, carefully open the packet (hot steam will shoot out!) and slide the salmon onto a serving platter. Serve with the mustard cream sauce.

2. Pour the chicken broth or wine over the fish. Bring the top and bottom edges of the foil together loosely to tent the fish and fold the sides to create a tightly sealed packet. Put it in the oven and bake for 10 to 15 minutes.

SHRIMP AND ROOTS STEW

This is sort of a cross between a chowder and a stew. It has milk and potatoes and onions. But it also has plenty of broth and other non-chowder type vegetables. No matter what you call it, serve this scrumptious and filling chowder/stew with crusty bread or large biscuits so you can get every last drop in the bowl.

HERE'S WHAT YOU NEED

3 tablespoons (42 g) unsalted butter, divided
1 tablespoon (15 ml) olive oil
1 small yellow onion, diced
2 celery stalks, diced
2 medium carrots, peeled and diced
2 medium parsnips, peeled and diced
1 large Yukon Gold potato, peeled and diced
2 teaspoons salt, divided
⅓ cup (42 g) all-purpose flour
3 cups (700 ml) chicken or vegetable broth
2 tablespoons (8 g) chopped fresh parsley, plus more for garnish
½ teaspoon ground black pepper
2 cups (475 ml) milk
1 pound (455 g) medium or large shrimp (41/50 or 31/35 count), cooked

HERE'S WHAT YOU GET

4 TO 6 STEWY, CHOWDERY SERVINGS

HERE'S WHAT YOU DO

1. In a large stockpot, melt 1 tablespoon (14 g) of the butter with the olive oil over medium-high heat. Add the onion and cook until softened, about 5 minutes.

2. Add the celery, carrots, parsnips, potatoes, and 1 teaspoon of the salt. Sauté, covered, for 15 minutes, stirring every few minutes.

4. Add the broth, parsley, the remaining 1 teaspoon of salt, and the pepper. Bring to a boil and then reduce the heat and simmer for 10 minutes.

3. Add the remaining 2 tablespoons (28 g) of butter. When it has melted, add the flour and mix well to incorporate (you don't want any lumps). Cook for 2 minutes.

5. Add the milk to the pot, return to a simmer (do not let it boil), and then add the shrimp. Cook for a minute or two, stirring a few times, to heat the shrimp.

6. Serve the stew hot, sprinkled with more parsley.

CLASSIC CRAB CAKES

If you're feeling flush, buy fresh crabmeat for these crab cakes. But otherwise, canned crabmeat works beautifully, too. This recipe adheres to the no–bell peppers school of thought. Some people have strong feelings about bell peppers in their crab cakes.

HERE'S WHAT YOU NEED

1 pound (455 g) crabmeat, picked over for shells and cartilage
3 tablespoons (42 g) mayonnaise
2 tablespoons (28 g) Dijon mustard
4 small scallions, thinly sliced (⅓ cup [33 g])
2 tablespoons (8 g) chopped fresh parsley
2 large eggs, lightly beaten
¾ cup (90 g) breadcrumbs
1 teaspoon salt
½ teaspoon ground black pepper
All-purpose flour, for dredging
2 tablespoons (28 ml) vegetable oil
Tartar sauce and lemon wedges, for serving

HERE'S WHAT YOU GET

8 CRAB CAKES TO SERVE 4 PEOPLE

HERE'S WHAT YOU DO

1. In a large bowl, mix the crabmeat, mayonnaise, mustard, scallions, and parsley, lightly tossing to evenly distribute all the ingredients.

A TASTY TIP To serve these in more of a Southern style, skip the tartar sauce and lemon wedges and put out a couple of different bottles of hot sauce instead.

2. Add the eggs, breadcrumbs, salt, and pepper, mixing gently but thoroughly to combine.

4. Put the flour in a shallow dish and carefully dredge each crab cake on both sides.

3. Divide the crabmeat mixture into 8 equal-size patties. Place the crab cakes on a baking sheet or platter and refrigerate for 20 minutes to let them firm up.

5. Heat the vegetable oil in a skillet that's large enough to hold all the crab cakes (or divide the oil between two skillets) and cook the crab cakes until golden, 4 to 5 minutes on each side.

6. Serve the crab cakes with tartar sauce and lemon wedges.

NO-DEEP-FRY FISH AND CHIPS

This fish is satisfyingly crunchy and rich, but without the deep frying. In terms of timing, bake the French fries ahead of time, set them aside, and then just warm them in the low oven at the end along with the cooked batches of fish. Or skip the fries altogether and serve the fish with chips, literally— potato chips, that is.

HERE'S WHAT YOU NEED

TARTAR SAUCE:

½ cup (115 g) mayonnaise

2 tablespoons (28 g) Dijon mustard

2 tablespoons (28 g) sweet or dill green relish

1 tablespoon (15 ml) fresh lemon juice

FISH:

1½ cups (188 g) all-purpose flour seasoned with 1 teaspoon each salt and ground black pepper

1½ cups (175 g) breadcrumbs seasoned with 1 teaspoon each salt and ground black pepper

2 large eggs, lightly beaten with 1 tablespoon (15 ml) water

1½ to 2 pounds (680 to 900 g) pollock or haddock, patted dry and cut into 3- to 4-inch (7.5 to 10 cm) chunks

Vegetable oil, for cooking

Your favorite French fries, prepared according to package directions

Lemon wedges, for serving

HERE'S WHAT YOU GET

4 TO 6 HEALTHIER SERVINGS OF FISH AND CHIPS

A TASTY TIP If you want to carry the "healthier" theme further, instead of cooking French fries ahead of time, roast some potato wedges in the oven instead. Season them as you like, set them aside while you cook the fish, and then warm them up quickly before serving, as you would with the fries.

HERE'S WHAT YOU DO

1. To make the tartar sauce, combine the mayonnaise, mustard, relish, and lemon juice in a bowl. Cover and refrigerate until ready to serve the fish. Preheat the oven to 200°F (93°C). Put the seasoned flour in a shallow bowl. Put the seasoned breadcrumbs in a second shallow bowl. Put the beaten eggs in a third shallow bowl and line them all up.

3. Heat 3 tablespoons (45 ml) of the vegetable oil in a large skillet over medium-high heat. When hot and shimmering, add the fish pieces to the skillet, without crowding, and cook the fish for 2 to 3 minutes per side until the breadcrumbs are set and golden. You will have to cook the fish in batches. Transfer the cooked fish to a paper towel–lined baking sheet and keep warm in the oven. Repeat until all the fish is cooked.

4. Serve the fish with the French fries, lemon wedges, and the tartar sauce.

2. Working with one piece at a time, dredge the fish first in the flour, then in the egg wash, letting any excess drip back into the bowl, and then finally in the breadcrumbs. Place the prepared fish on a plate.

BAKED COD ON A BED OF VEGETABLES

This satisfying one-dish meal is hearty, and healthy, and homey all at once. The thinly sliced onions, potatoes, and tomatoes all meld together in the oven, infusing each other with their flavors. The cod fillets stay moist and flaky. And because it's all done in one dish, cleanup is a snap.

HERE'S WHAT YOU NEED

1 large yellow or white onion, very thinly sliced

3 large Yukon Gold potatoes, peeled and cut into slices ¼-inch (6 mm) thick

3 medium tomatoes, sliced ½-inch (1.3 cm) thick

Salt and ground black pepper to taste

1 cup (235 ml) vegetable or chicken broth, divided

1½ pounds (680 g) cod fillets (or any other thick white fish)

2 tablespoons (28 g) unsalted butter, cut into small pieces

2 tablespoons (5 cm) chopped fresh basil, plus more for garnish

HERE'S WHAT YOU GET

4 TO 6 ONE-DISH SERVINGS

HERE'S WHAT YOU DO

1. Preheat the oven to 350°F (180°C, or gas mark 4). Lightly grease a 9 x 13-inch (23 x 33 cm) baking dish. In the dish, layer first the onion, then the potatoes, and finally the tomatoes. Sprinkle ½ teaspoon of salt and ½ teaspoon of pepper between each layer of vegetables.

3. Take the baking dish out of the oven, uncover, and place the fish fillets on top of the vegetables. Sprinkle with ½ teaspoon of salt and ½ teaspoon of pepper. Drizzle with the remaining ½ cup (120 ml) of broth, dot with the butter pieces, and scatter the basil over the top.

2. Drizzle the vegetables with ½ cup (120 ml) of the broth, cover the dish with aluminum foil, and bake for 20 to 25 minutes until the potatoes are fork-tender.

4. Cover with aluminum foil and bake for 15 to 20 minutes more (depending on thickness of the fish) until the fish is cooked all the way through.

5. Serve the fish and vegetables with all of the delicious accumulated juices. Garnish each serving with basil.

SWEETS FOR DESSERT— OR ANYTIME

PECAN-CHOCOLATE CHIP COOKIES

These classic chocolate chip cookies are dressed up a bit with pecans. This nut has a nice buttery quality that works well in a cookie (or other baked goods), but feel free to substitute chopped walnuts or almonds, if you like. This recipe makes a lot of cookies, so you'll need to bake the cookies in two batches.

HERE'S WHAT YOU NEED

1 cup (2 sticks, or 225 g) unsalted butter, softened
¾ cup (170 g) packed light brown sugar
¾ cup (150 g) granulated sugar
2 teaspoons vanilla extract
2 large eggs
2¼ cups (281 g) all-purpose flour
1 teaspoon baking soda
1 teaspoon salt
2 cups (350 g) semisweet chocolate chips
1 cup (110 g) chopped pecans

HERE'S WHAT YOU GET

42 TO 48 CHOCOLATEY COOKIES

HERE'S WHAT YOU DO

1. Preheat the oven to 350°F (180°C, or gas mark 4). Line baking sheets with parchment paper. With a handheld or standing electric mixer, cream together the butter and both sugars until they are soft and incorporated.

2. Add the vanilla and then the eggs, one a time, beating until everything is combined.

3. Mix the flour, baking soda, and salt in a bowl and then beat them into the mixture.

4. With a rubber spatula, mix in the chocolate chips and pecans.

5. Drop the batter by large spoonfuls onto the baking sheets, placing 12 mounds per baking sheet. Bake the cookies for 10 minutes until the tops are golden.

6. Let the cookies cool on the baking sheets for 5 minutes and then transfer them to a wire cooling rack.

TRIPLE THREAT CHOCOLATE CUPCAKES

These cupcakes use cocoa powder in both the cakes and the frosting, as well as unsweetened chocolate, for a triple chocolate punch. So, using good-quality cocoa powder is important. Good old Hershey's natural cocoa (or Hershey's Special Dark cocoa) will make fabulous cupcakes that will remind you of the hot cocoa you loved as a kid. Or use a premium cocoa powder like Valrhona, Guittard, or Callebaut.

HERE'S WHAT YOU NEED

CUPCAKES:
2 cups (400 g) granulated sugar
1½ cups (188 g) all-purpose flour
¾ teaspoon baking soda
¼ teaspoon salt
1 cup (235 ml) unsweetened hot cocoa prepared with milk, hot
½ cup (115 g) sour cream
½ cup (120 ml) vegetable oil
2 large eggs, at room temperature
4 ounces (115 g) unsweetened chocolate, melted
FROSTING:
2¾ cups (330 g) confectioners' sugar, sifted
6 tablespoons (30 g) unsweetened cocoa powder
6 tablespoons (85 g) unsalted butter, softened
5 tablespoons (75 ml) heavy cream
1 teaspoon vanilla extract

HERE'S WHAT YOU GET

18 COCOA-PACKED CUPCAKES

HERE'S WHAT YOU DO

1. Preheat the oven to 350°F (180°C, or gas mark 4). Line 18 wells of muffin pans with paper cupcake liners. To make the cupcakes, in a large bowl, sift together sugar, flour, baking soda, and salt. In another bowl, whisk together the prepared hot cocoa, sour cream, and vegetable oil.

2. Slowly whisk the liquid ingredients into the dry ingredients.

4. Divide the batter among the prepared muffin cups, using about ⅓ cup (85 g) batter per cupcake. Bake for 20 to 25 minutes until a toothpick inserted in the middle of a cupcake comes out clean. Let the cupcakes cool in the muffin pans for 5 minutes and then remove and let cool on wire cooling racks.

3. Add the eggs, one at a time, whisking until combined, followed by the melted chocolate. Whisk until everything is smooth and evenly combined.

5. To make the frosting, whisk together the confectioners' sugar, cocoa powder, butter, cream, and vanilla until the frosting is completely combined and smooth.

6. When the cupcakes are completely cool, frost the cupcakes using a butter knife or small spatula.

GINGERY PEAR CRISP

Here's a little secret: Fruit crisps make wonderful and easy desserts, but they also make superb breakfasts. Yes, there's some sugar, but there's also lots of fruit! And oats! Skip the whipped cream or ice cream, though, if serving for breakfast. We do have to make some concessions, after all.

HERE'S WHAT YOU NEED

6 cups (966 g) chopped pears
   (1-inch, or 2.5 cm cubes)
⅓ cup (67 g) granulated sugar
¼ cup (24 g) chopped candied ginger
1 teaspoon grated lemon zest
1 tablespoon (15 ml) fresh lemon juice
1 cup (90 g) quick-cooking oats
⅓ cup (75 g) packed light brown sugar
2 tablespoons (13 g) almond meal
½ teaspoon ground cinnamon
½ teaspoon ground ginger
4 tablespoons (55 g) unsalted butter, cut into
   small pieces, cold, plus more for preparing the
   baking dish or pie plate
Whipped cream or ice cream, for serving

HERE'S WHAT YOU GET

6 TO 8 DESSERT (OR BREAKFAST . . .) SERVINGS

A TASTY TIP Peel the pears or not, according to your preference and what type of pears you buy for this crisp. Bartlett pears have tender skins and don't need peeling, but Anjou and Bosc pears have tougher skins, so you might want to peel those.

HERE'S WHAT YOU DO

1. Preheat the oven to 375°F (190°C, or gas mark 5). Butter an 8-inch (20 cm) square baking dish or a deep-dish 9-inch (23 cm) pie plate. In a large bowl, combine the pears, sugar, candied ginger, lemon zest, and lemon juice.

3. In a bowl, combine the oats, brown sugar, almond meal, cinnamon, and ground ginger. Mix in the cold butter pieces by cutting and mashing them in with a fork until the whole thing becomes a crumbly mixture that holds together. It's okay to still see little streaks of butter.

2. Transfer the pear mixture to the prepared baking dish.

4. Sprinkle the topping mixture over the pears. Bake the crisp for 25 to 30 minutes until the top is lightly browned and the pears are bubbly.

5. Serve warm, with whipped cream or ice cream.

COCOA AND CHOCOLATE BROWNIES

Everyone should have a good cocoa powder brownie recipe in their kitchen repertoire. It is so much easier than melting solid chocolate, and do we really have to say that it's infinitely superior to a boxed brownie mix? Using cocoa creates a moist, dense, fudgy brownie with a crackly top—or in other words, brownie nirvana.

HERE'S WHAT YOU NEED

¾ cup (1½ sticks, or 165 g) unsalted butter
1 tablespoon (15 ml) vanilla extract
1 cup (200 g) granulated sugar
1 cup (225 g) packed dark brown sugar
1¼ cups (100 g) unsweetened cocoa powder
2 large eggs
½ cup (63 g) all-purpose flour
¼ teaspon of salt
1 cup (175 g) semisweet chocolate chips

HERE'S WHAT YOU GET

16 GOOEY BROWNIES

HERE'S WHAT YOU DO

1. Preheat the oven to 350°F (180°C, or gas mark 4). Prepare an 8-inch (20 cm) baking pan by cutting two 7 x 11-inch (18 x 28 cm) pieces of parchment paper and arranging them in the baking pan, crisscrossing them to create an overhang. This will make it much easier to remove the brownies from the pan.

2. In a saucepan over medium-low heat, melt the butter and then add the vanilla, both sugars, and the cocoa powder. Mix until all the ingredients come together into a thick paste.

4. Add the flour and salt and beat until everything is combined. (Be careful not to overmix here; you don't want to incorporate too much air into the batter.) With a spatula or wooden spoon, stir in the chocolate chips.

3. Remove from the heat and let the cocoa mixture cool for 5 minutes. Using a handheld electric mixer, beat in the eggs, one at a time.

5. Pour the batter into the prepared pan and bake for 20 to 25 minutes until toothpick dipped in center emerges slightly moist with batter. Let the brownies cool for 10 minutes in the pan and then use the parchment paper overhang to remove the brownie slab from the pan.

6. Cut the brownies into 16 squares.

ALMOST LIKE MOM'S APPLE PIE

For a lot of people, even experienced cooks, the thought of making a piecrust from scratch incites a mild form of dread. There's a lot of pressure to deliver a flaky, light crust with no "soggy bottoms," as Mary Berry from *The Great British Baking Show* would say. Well, Mary might not approve of a store-bought crust, but once you serve this pie—to great acclaim—you will approve, and that's what matters.

HERE'S WHAT YOU NEED

1 package prepared pie dough (for a double-crust pie)
6 Granny Smith apples, peeled, cored, and sliced into ¼-inch-thick pieces (7 to 8 cups, or 770 to 880 g)
1 teaspoon grated lemon zest
1 tablespoon (15 ml) fresh lemon juice
½ cup (115 g) packed dark brown sugar
3 tablespoons (24 g) all-purpose flour
1 teaspoon ground cinnamon
½ teaspoon ground ginger
½ teaspoon ground cardamom
¼ teaspoon ground nutmeg
2 tablespoons (28 g) unsalted butter, cut into 8 pieces, cold
1 large egg, beaten
1½ teaspoons granulated sugar

HERE'S WHAT YOU GET

6 TO 8 FLAKY, APPLY SERVINGS

HERE'S WHAT YOU DO

1. Preheat the oven to 450°F (230°C, or gas mark 8). Line a 9-inch (23 cm) deep-dish pie plate with one layer of the dough, patting in the bottom and up the sides and letting it overhang the edges slightly. Refrigerate until ready to use.

2. In a large bowl, toss the apples with the lemon zest and lemon juice. Add the brown sugar, flour, cinnamon, ginger, cardamom, and nutmeg, tossing everything thoroughly and covering all the apple slices with the dry ingredients.

4. Cover the apples with the second piece of dough, sealing the edges with a bit of water on your fingers and crimping the edges with your fingers or a fork. Put the whole thing back in the refrigerator for 15 minutes to chill.

3. Carefully transfer the apples into the pie dish, spreading them evenly. Dot with the pieces of cold butter.

5. Brush the top of the pie with the beaten egg and sprinkle the top with the granulated sugar. Cut a couple of slashes in the top crust. Bake for 10 minutes. Lower the heat to 350°F (180°C, or gas mark 4) and bake for 20 minutes more. Cover with loosely tented aluminum foil (as the pie will brown quickly at this point and you don't want the crust to burn) and bake for 20 minutes more. The crust should be golden brown and the apple filling should be bubbling up through the slashes in the crust.

6. Let your beautiful finished pie cool for 15 minutes before cutting into slices.

NOT YOUR TYPICAL OATMEAL COOKIES

These hearty cookies have an unexpected and colorful surprise: Bright red dried cranberries and creamy white chocolate chips add a tart-sweet pop of flavor to the toasty, nutty oatmeal cookie base.

HERE'S WHAT YOU NEED

¾ cup (1½ sticks, or 165 g) unsalted butter, softened
¾ cup (170 g) packed light brown sugar
½ cup (100 g) granulated sugar
1 teaspoon vanilla extract
2 large eggs
1½ cups (188 g) all-purpose flour
1 teaspoon baking soda
1 teaspoon ground cinnamon
3 cups (288 g) old-fashioned rolled oats
1 cup (120 g) dried cranberries
1 cup (170 g) white chocolate chips

HERE'S WHAT YOU GET

ABOUT 36 CREATIVE COOKIES

HERE'S WHAT YOU DO

1. Preheat the oven to 350°F (180°C, or gas mark 4). Line baking sheets with parchment paper. Using a handheld electric mixer, beat the butter and both sugars together until creamy.

A TASTY TIP Load up these cookies by adding 1 cup (100 g) chopped almonds, (115 g) hazelnuts, or (110 g) pecans along with the chocolate chips and cranberries.

2. Add the vanilla and beat in the eggs, one at a time, until incorporated.

4. Add the oats, cranberries, and chocolate chips, stirring with a spatula to make sure they are well distributed throughout the batter.

3. Mix in the flour, baking soda, and cinnamon until everything is incorporated.

5. Drop the batter by large spoonfuls onto the prepared baking sheets, placing 12 cookies per baking sheet. Bake for 8 to 10 minutes until the cookies are set and the tops are turning golden.

6. Let the cookies cool for 5 minutes on the baking sheets and then transfer the cookies to a wire cooling rack. Serve warm or at room temperature.

FROM-SCRATCH GRANOLA BARS

Homemade granola bars rock because you control how much sugar and other ingredients go into them. This recipe is forgiving, so you can play around a bit: Use crunchy or smooth peanut butter, sweetened or unsweetened coconut, unsalted or salted pepitas, sunflower seeds instead of pepitas, or sub in milk chocolate chips or bittersweet chocolate chips for the semisweet. Just keep the proportion of wet ingredients to dry ingredients the same.

HERE'S WHAT YOU NEED

¾ cup (195 g) peanut butter
½ cup (1 stick, or 112 g) unsalted butter
½ cup (115 g) packed dark brown sugar
⅓ cup (115 g) honey
2 tablespoons (28 ml) vanilla extract
2½ cups (240 g) old-fashioned rolled oats
1 cup (92 g) sliced almonds
¾ cup (131 g) semisweet chocolate chips
½ cup (69 g) pepitas (pumpkin seeds)
½ cup (40 g) shredded coconut
½ cup (50 g) almond meal
¼ cup (36 g) sesame seeds
½ teaspoon ground cinnamon
½ teaspoon salt

HERE'S WHAT YOU GET

ABOUT 36 HEALTHY HOMEMADE SERVINGS

HERE'S WHAT YOU DO

1. Preheat the oven to 350°F (180°C, or gas mark 4). Cut parchment paper to a size 12½ x 16 inches (31 x 40 cm) and line the 9 x 13-inch (23 x 33 cm) baking pan with the paper. (You want extra paper hanging over the edges so that you can use it to remove the granola slab after baking.) In a large saucepan over low heat, melt together the peanut butter, butter, brown sugar, honey, and vanilla. Watch carefully so that nothing starts to burn.

3. Remove the peanut butter mixture from the heat and let cool slightly. Then mix it into the dried ingredients with a rubber spatula, making sure they are all distributed evenly and evenly coated with the liquid ingredients.

2. In a large bowl, mix the oats, almonds, chocolate chips, pepitas, coconut, almond meal, sesame seeds, cinnamon, and salt.

4. Transfer the mixture to the prepared baking pan and press it in using your clean hands until it is a uniform thickness. If necessary to prevent sticking, wet your hands slightly.

5. Bake for 20 to 25 minutes until the edges start to brown. Let the granola slab cool to room temperature and then cut into bars or squares.

COCONUT MACAROONS

If you ever happen to be in New York City on March 20, keep an eye out for local bakeries offering free macaroons for the city's Macaroon Day, a celebration started a few years back by pastry chef (and cookie genius) François Payard. Or, make your own macaroons at home on May 31 to commemorate National Macaroon Day.

HERE'S WHAT YOU NEED

14 ounces (390 g) unsweetened flaked coconut

1 can (14 ounces, or 390 g) of sweetened condensed milk

1 teaspoon vanilla extract

2 large egg whites, at room temperature

¼ teaspoon salt

25 whole almonds

½ cup (88 g) semisweet chocolate chips

HERE'S WHAT YOU GET

25 CHEWY MACAROONS

A TASTY TIP You can make these macaroons chocolaty throughout by adding about ¼ cup (20 g) of unsweetened cocoa powder to the coconut-milk mixture in step 1.

HERE'S WHAT YOU DO

1. Preheat the oven to 350°F (180°C, or gas mark 4). Line 2 baking sheets with parchment paper. In a large bowl, combine the coconut, condensed milk, and vanilla, making sure the coconut is completely coated with the condensed milk.

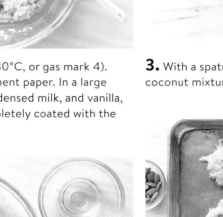

2. Using a handheld or standing electric mixer, beat the egg whites and salt on high speed until they hold medium-soft peaks (the peaks will just start to hold their shape, but will melt back into themselves after a second or two).

3. With a spatula, gently fold the egg whites into the coconut mixture until well combined.

4. Drop the mixture into 2-inch (5 cm) balls on the baking sheets. Gently place an almond in the middle of each mound. Bake for 25 to 30 minutes until just golden brown.

5. Let the macaroons cool on the baking sheets. Melt the chocolate in a bowl in the microwave in 30-second increments, stirring between each time. Drizzle the melted chocolate over the macaroons and let the chocolate set.

SPICED POACHED PEARS

These highly spiced poached pears are an extremely elegant way to end a meal. The combination of spices gives the pears an almost pie-like flavor. Feel free to try orange zest and juice instead of the lemon for a gentler citrus taste.

HERE'S WHAT YOU NEED

4 Bosc pears (ripe but still firm)
4 cups (950 ml) water
2 cups (400 g) sugar
7 whole cloves
5 whole cardamom pods
1 cinnamon stick
1-inch (2.5 cm) chunk fresh ginger, peeled and cut in half
1 long strand of lemon zest (from about ½ of a lemon)
Juice of 1 lemon
1 tablespoon (15 ml) vanilla extract
Whipped cream, for serving (optional)

HERE'S WHAT YOU GET

4 TO 8 SOPHISTICATED SERVINGS

A TASTY TIP These poached pears are also delicious served chilled. After you take them off the stove, let them come to room temperature and then refrigerate the pears in their liquid for serving later.

HERE'S WHAT YOU DO

1. Slice the pears in half lengthwise and, using a teaspoon, remove the cores. (You can peel them if you like, although leaving the peels on will help the pears hold together. It is your choice.)

3. Add the pears, arranging them cut-side up, and simmer, uncovered, for 20 minutes or until the pears are tender. Occasionally, baste the pears with the poaching liquid.

4. Take the skillet off the heat and let the pears stand in the hot liquid until ready to serve. Top the pears with a bit of the poaching liquid and a dollop of whipped cream, if you like.

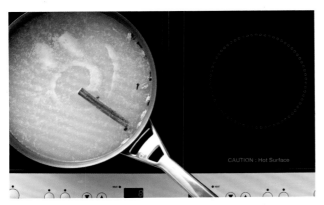

2. In a large deep skillet (not nonstick) over medium heat, bring the water and sugar to a low simmer to dissolve the sugar. Add the cloves, cardamom, cinnamon stick, ginger, lemon zest, lemon juice, and vanilla and bring back to a simmer.

STRAWBERRY SHORTCAKES

Because this recipe is so simple and it's so all about the strawberries, try to find the freshest, ripest berries in your market. Or better yet—if you can—pick your own. This is a great dessert to serve at a summer barbecue: You can just set up a station with the plate of biscuits, a big bowl of berries, and the whipped cream and let everyone make their own shortcakes.

HERE'S WHAT YOU NEED

8 cups (1.2 kg) fresh strawberries, cut in half
2 to 4 tablespoons (26 to 50 g) sugar, as needed
2 tablespoons (28 ml) fresh lemon juice
1 tablespoon (15 ml) vanilla extract
12 biscuits (store-bought, or make your own)
Whipped cream, for serving

HERE'S WHAT YOU GET

6 SUMMERY SERVINGS

Variation

When blackberries are in season, make blackberry shortcakes. Put the berries in a bowl, mash some of them for maximum juiciness, and then add the sugar and other ingredients and proceed with the recipe as directed.

HERE'S WHAT YOU DO

1. About an hour before you're ready to serve dessert, mix the strawberries in a bowl with the sugar, lemon juice, and vanilla. Let sit, stirring every once in a while. This will allow the strawberries to get really juicy and wonderful. You could also do this a couple of hours before serving, refrigerating the berries.

3. Spoon a generous dollop of whipped cream on top. Spoon some strawberries with their accumulated juices over the whipped cream and cover with the biscuit top.

4. Serve with additional strawberries and whipped cream on the side.

2. When ready to serve, split the biscuits in half horizontally with a serrated knife and place the bottom part of each biscuit on a plate.

APRICOT CLAFOUTIS

A clafoutis is a rustic-but-elegant baked dessert, originating in France, of fruit arranged in a buttered dish and covered with a thick, custardy batter. The whole thing is then baked to fluffy golden perfection. Cherries are the traditional choice, but apricots make a more delicate, beautifully fragrant clafoutis. You could use any other summer fruit that's not excessively juicy, like blueberries or blackberries.

HERE'S WHAT YOU NEED

10 to 12 ripe apricots, cut in half and pitted

⅓ cup (67 g) plus 2 tablespoons (26 g) granulated sugar, divided

½ cup (63 g) all-purpose flour

1¼ cups (285 ml) milk

4 large eggs

1 tablespoon (14 g) unsalted butter, softened, plus more for preparing the quiche or tart pan

Pinch of salt

Confectioners' sugar, for dusting

HERE'S WHAT YOU GET

6 TO 8 SIMPLE BUT IMPRESSIVE SERVINGS

A TASTY TIP Clafoutis are best eaten the same day they are baked, either warm or at room temperature.

HERE'S WHAT YOU DO

1. Preheat the oven to 350°F (180°C, or gas mark 4). Butter a 10-inch (25 cm) wide and 2-inch (5 cm) deep quiche or tart pan. Line the bottom of the pan with the apricot halves. Evenly sprinkle the 2 tablespoons (26 g) of granulated sugar over the apricots.

3. Slowly and carefully pour the batter mixture over the apricots.

2. Put the remaining ⅓ cup (67 g) of granulated sugar, the flour, milk, eggs, butter, and salt in a blender and blend on high speed for about 1 minute, or until all the ingredients are blended into what looks like a homogeneous smoothielike liquid.

4. Bake on the middle rack of the oven for 45 minutes or until a knife insert in the middle comes out clean. Let the clafoutis cool for 10 minutes on a wire cooling rack.

5. Dust with confectioners' sugar just before serving.

MIXED BERRY COULIS

A coulis can be either sweet, with fruit, or savory, with vegetables. Traditionally, this French sauce is strained to make it super-smooth, but we're not going to bother with that here. Serve this endlessly versatile dessert sauce over ice cream, yogurt, pound cake, or panna cotta. Or use it at breakfast time as a topping for pancakes, waffles, corn muffins, or oatmeal.

HERE'S WHAT YOU NEED

6 cups (weight will vary) fresh or frozen mixed berries, such as blueberries, strawberries, raspberries, and/or blackberries

¾ cup (175 ml) white grape juice

2 tablespoons (28 ml) fresh lemon juice

¼ cup (50 g) sugar

1 tablespoon (7 g) ground cinnamon

½ teaspoon freshly cracked black pepper

¼ teaspoon fine sea salt

HERE'S WHAT YOU GET

3 CUPS OF COULIS

A TASTY TIP You could make this with just one kind of berry, if you like, for an intense single-flavor sauce. Or try it with really juicy summer peaches or nectarines (peel them first).

HERE'S WHAT YOU DO

1. In a large saucepan, stir together the berries, grape juice, lemon juice, sugar, cinnamon, cracked pepper, and salt. Bring to a boil.

3. Taste the sauce and adjust the seasoning if you like, with more lemon, spices, etc.

4. Serve the coulis right away or store in an airtight glass container in the refrigerator until ready to serve.

2. Reduce the heat to a simmer and cook the berries for 15 to 20 minutes until they have broken down. Remove the pan from the stove and let cool to room temperature.

INTENSE FLOURLESS CHOCOLATE CAKE

Use the best-quality chocolate you can here and serve this luxe, rich cake in small slices. For neat-looking slices, dip a very sharp knife into hot water and then wipe it dry between every slice.

HERE'S WHAT YOU NEED

1 cup (2 sticks, or 225 g) unsalted butter, cut into 8 pieces, plus more for preparing the cake pan
Unsweetened cocoa powder, for dusting
8 ounces (225 g) bittersweet chocolate, chopped
1 cup (200 g) sugar
4 large eggs
Whipped cream, for serving

HERE'S WHAT YOU GET

8 DARK, INTENSE SERVINGS

HERE'S WHAT YOU DO

1. Preheat the oven to 350°F (180°C, or gas mark 4). Butter the bottom and sides of a 9-inch (23 cm) round cake pan. Cut out a 9-inch (23 cm) circle of parchment paper to line the bottom of the pan. Butter the paper and then dust it with 2 tablespoons (10 g) of the cocoa powder. Set aside. Set up a double boiler over medium heat or set a heatproof bowl over a saucepan filled with an inch or two (2.5 to 5 cm) of water (don't let the bottom of the bowl touch the water). Bring the water in the bottom to a simmer and melt the chocolate, butter, and sugar together in the top, stirring until smooth.

2. Remove the top pan or the bowl from the double boiler. With a handheld electric mixer, beat the eggs into the chocolate mixture, one at a time, making sure the mixture stays smooth.

4. Carefully remove the setup from the oven. Carefully transfer the cake pan from the hot water to a wire cooling rack and let cool completely. Once cool, cover the cake loosely with plastic wrap and refrigerate for 3 hours, or up to overnight.

3. Transfer the chocolate batter into the prepared cake pan. Place the cake pan into a small roasting pan (or other pan with sides) and place this setup in the oven. Carefully pour a couple of inches (5 cm) of very hot tap water into the roasting pan, being careful not to splash any into the batter. Bake the cake for 1 hour.

5. Remove the cake from the pan by running a hot knife around the edge and dipping the bottom of the pan into hot water. Turn the pan out onto a cutting board, giving it a good bang to release the cake. Put the cake on a plate and carefully peel off the parchment paper. Refrigerate until ready to serve.

6. When ready to serve, let the cake sit at room temperature for 30 to 45 minutes. Using a fine-mesh sifter, dust cocoa powder over the entire surface of the cake. Serve with whipped cream.

WHITE PEPPERMINT BARK

Make big batches of this incredibly easy peppermint bark to give at the holidays as gifts or to have around when company comes over. You can of course substitute semisweet chocolate chips for the white chocolate chips, if you'd rather. Or make batches of both!

HERE'S WHAT YOU NEED

6 ounces (170 g) hard peppermint candy or candy canes
2 pounds (900 g) white chocolate chips
1 tablespoon (15 ml) peppermint extract

HERE'S WHAT YOU GET

ABOUT 2¼ POUNDS (1 KG) OF MINTY BARK

HERE'S WHAT YOU DO

1. Cover a large baking sheet with parchment paper or waxed paper. In a food processor, chop the peppermint candy into small pieces by pulsing the machine on and off.

3. Remove the top of the double boiler from the heat and stir the peppermint extract into the melted chocolate. Stir in the chopped peppermint candy.

2. Set up a double boiler over medium heat or set a heatproof bowl over a saucepan filled with an inch or two (2.5 to 5 cm) of water (don't let the bottom of the bowl touch the water). Bring the water in the bottom to a simmer and melt the white chocolate chips, stirring as needed, until smooth and glossy.

4. Quickly pour the mixture onto the prepared baking sheet, spreading the mixture to an even thickness over the entire baking sheet with a spatula.

5. Transfer the baking sheet to the refrigerator until set, about 30 minutes. When ready, cut or break the bark into serving pieces.

CHOCOLATE CHIP BREAD PUDDING

You can use just about any type of bread you like for bread pudding. Brioche or challah will soak up the custard like a delicious sponge. In New Orleans, where bread pudding is practically an art form, leftover French bread is the first choice. You could even use leftover croissants, should you find yourself in that situation.

HERE'S WHAT YOU NEED

2 tablespoons (28 g) unsalted butter

4 to 5 cups (200 to 250 g) bread cubes (cut or torn into 1-inch, or 2.5 cm pieces)

4 cups (950 ml) milk, warmed

4 large eggs

1 cup (200 g) sugar

1 teaspoon vanilla extract

½ cup (88 g) semisweet chocolate chips

HERE'S WHAT YOU GET

8 TO 10 RICH SERVINGS

A TASTY TIP Using day old-bread or cutting the fresh bread into cubes and letting it sit out for a couple of hours will help the bread absorb the custard better, leading to a tastier bread pudding.

HERE'S WHAT YOU DO

1. Preheat the oven to 350°F (180°C, or gas mark 4). Butter a 9 x 13-inch (23 x 33 cm) baking dish. Layer the bread cubes evenly in the baking dish.

3. Pour the milk mixture over the bread cubes in the baking dish. Let it sit in the refridgerator for about 30 minutes to let the egg mixture soak into the bread. Sprinkle the top with the chocolate chips.

4. Bake the bread pudding for 45 minutes until a knife inserted an inch (2.5 cm) from the edge comes out clean. Let cool for about 10 minutes before cutting. Serve warm.

2. In a large bowl, whisk the milk, eggs, sugar, and vanilla until smooth.

THE SIMPLEST CHOCOLATE MOUSSE

Sometimes cream is incorporated into chocolate mousse for richness, but here it's the richness of the chocolate that does the talking. The mousse is lightened by folding in beaten egg whites. Since there are so few ingredients here, use the absolute best quality you can buy.

HERE'S WHAT YOU NEED

4 ounces (115 g) bittersweet chocolate
1 tablespoon (14 g) unsalted butter
4 large eggs, separated, at room temperature

HERE'S WHAT YOU GET

4 TO 6 LIGHT AND AIRY SERVINGS

A TASTY TIP Experiment with adding different flavorings to the melted chocolate-butter mixture: several pinches of a ground spice like cinnamon or cardamom, or a bit of instant espresso powder, or a few drops of vanilla or orange extract.

HERE'S WHAT YOU DO

1. Set up a double boiler over medium heat or set a heat-proof bowl over a saucepan filled with an inch or two (2.5 to 5 cm) of water (don't let the bottom of the bowl touch the water). Bring the water in the bottom to a simmer. In the top, melt the chocolate and butter together, stirring, until smooth.

3. In another large bowl, beat the egg whites until stiff peaks form. (Use a whisk or a handheld electric mixer.)

2. Take the top of the double boiler off the heat and mix in the egg yolks, one at a time, until totally combined. Transfer the mixture to a large bowl.

4. Slowly and gently fold the beaten egg whites into the chocolate mixture just until they are all incorporated and no white streaks remain.

5. Pour the mousse into a serving bowl or into 4 to 6 individual small serving bowls or ramekins. Chill for at least 1 hour before serving.

PERFECT CRÈME BRÛLÉE

Silky-smooth custard topped with crunchy caramelized sugar that shatters with a light touch of your spoon is a miraculous thing and a study in contrasts. It's fun to play with a kitchen torch if you have one, but it's just as easy to caramelize the sugar under the oven broiler. Whichever method you choose, make sure the custard is cold before you start to caramelize the sugar or else you will end up with crème brûlée soup.

HERE'S WHAT YOU NEED

8 large egg yolks
⅓ cup (67 g) plus 4 tablespoons (50 g) sugar, divided
2 cups (475 ml) heavy cream
1 teaspoon vanilla extract

HERE'S WHAT YOU GET

6 CRISPY-TOPPED CREAMY CUSTARDS

HERE'S WHAT YOU DO

1. Preheat the oven to 300°F (150°C, or gas mark 2). In a large bowl, whisk together the egg yolks and ⅓ cup (67 g) of the sugar until the sugar has dissolved and the mixture is thick and pale yellow. Add the cream and vanilla and continue whisking until well blended.

2. Divide the mixture among 6 ovenproof ramekins or custard cups. Place a clean kitchen towel in a shallow roasting pan or baking dish. Place the ramekins on the towel and slowly pour hot tap water into the pan around the ramekins, being careful not to splash any water into the ramekins. Bring the water level halfway up the sides of the ramekins.

3. Carefully transfer this setup to the oven and bake until the custard is set around the edges but still wobbly in the center, 40 to 50 minutes. Remove the roasting pan from the oven and leave the ramekins in their water bath until cool.

4. Remove the ramekins from the water and chill in the refrigerator to firm up for at least 2 hours or up to 2 days. When ready to serve, sprinkle 2 teaspoons of the remaining sugar over each custard.

5. For the best results, use a small handheld kitchen torch to melt the sugar; you want it to turn brown. Or preheat the oven broiler, arrange the ramekins on a baking sheet, and place under the broiler until the sugar melts, watching carefully so they brown but don't burn.

6. Re-chill the custards for about 10 minutes before serving.

NO-FUSS PEACH GALETTE

You could call a galette a lazy person's pie. Or to be more diplomatic, you could call it a novice baker's pie. With this freeform creation, the more rustic it looks, the better. It is leaps and bounds less stressful than baking a pie, and you'll get all the same accolades as if you had actually made a pie. What's not to love about that?

HERE'S WHAT YOU NEED

DOUGH:

1 cup (125 g) all-purpose flour

2 tablespoons (26 g) sugar

½ teaspoon ground cardamom

½ teaspoon ground cinnamon

¼ teaspoon salt

½ cup (1 stick, or 112 g) unsalted butter, cut into small pieces, cold

3 tablespoons (45 ml) ice water

FILLING:

¼ cup (31 g) all-purpose flour

¼ cup (50 g) sugar

½ teaspoon ground cinnamon

½ teaspoon ground cardamom

Pinch of salt

4 peaches, peeled, cut in half then ¼-inch (6 mm) slices

Grated zest and juice of ½ of a lemon

2 tablespoons (28 g) unsalted butter, cut into small pieces, cold

HERE'S WHAT YOU DO

1. To make the dough, put the flour, sugar, cardamom, cinnamon, and salt in a food processor to blend everything. Scatter the cold butter pieces on top and pulse a few times until the mixture looks like coarse cornmeal. With the motor running, pour in the ice water and let the mixture come together into a dough.

HERE'S WHAT YOU GET

6 TO 8 STRESS-FREE SLICES

4. On a piece of parchment paper, roll out the dough into an 11-inch (28 cm) round. Transfer the peach mixture to the dough, spreading it out evenly and leaving a 2-inch (5 cm) border of dough all around the edge.

2. Invert the mixture onto a clean surface, form it into a ball, flatten the ball into a disk, wrap the disk in plastic, and let the dough rest in the refrigerator for at least 1 hour or up to 2 days.

5. Scatter the cold butter on top of the peaches. Carefully fold in the dough border over the peaches to partially cover them but leaving an exposed part in the middle.

6. Transfer the galette along with the parchment to a baking sheet and refrigerate for 20 minutes. Meanwhile, preheat the oven to 400°F (200°C, or gas mark 6). Bake the galette for 20 to 30 minutes until the crust is nice and golden and the exposed filling is bubbling. Let cool on a wire cooling rack, cut into slices, and serve warm or at room temperature.

3. To make the filling, in a large bowl, mix the flour, sugar, cinnamon, cardamom, and salt. Add the sliced peaches to the mixture and toss gently to coat them evenly. Add the lemon zest and lemon juice and toss again. Set the filling aside while you roll the dough.

SOUR CREAM CHOCOLATE CHIP NUT LOAF

This is somewhat reminiscent of a coffee cake in terms of its flavor and texture (but there's no crumb topping). Yes, it's in the dessert chapter, but there's something about baking a cake in a loaf shape that encourages you to indulge in a slice at really any time of day, don't you think?

HERE'S WHAT YOU NEED

½ cup (1 stick, or 112 g) unsalted butter, plus more for preparing the baking pan

1 cup (200 g) sugar

3 large eggs, separated

3 tablespoons (18 g) grated lemon zest

2 cups (250 g) all-purpose flour

1 teaspoon baking soda

1 teaspoon baking powder

¼ teaspoon salt

1 cup (230 g) sour cream

1 pound (455 g) semisweet chocolate chips

1 cup (120 g) chopped walnuts

HERE'S WHAT YOU GET

A 9-INCH (23 CM) LOAF CAKE FOR ANYTIME SNACKING

HERE'S WHAT YOU DO

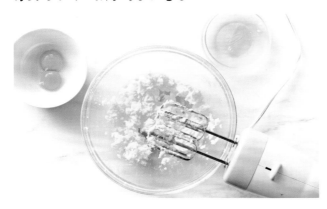

1. Preheat the oven to 350°F (180°C, or gas mark 4). Grease a 9-inch (23 cm) loaf pan with butter. With a handheld mixer or a standing mixer, cream together the butter and sugar until light and fluffy. One at a time, beat in the egg yolks until combined. Beat in the lemon zest.

3. In a separate clean bowl, beat the egg whites until stiff peaks form. Using a spatula, fold the beaten egg whites into the batter mixture. Fold in the chocolate chips and walnuts with the spatula.

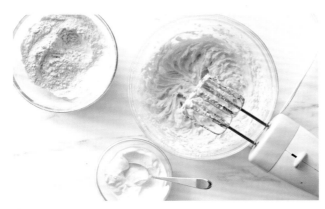

2. Sift together the flour, baking soda, baking powder, and salt. Add this mixture to the butter-egg mixture in batches, alternating it with adding the sour cream and beating to incorporate everything after each addition.

4. Pour the batter into the prepared loaf pan and bake for 45 to 50 minutes until a knife inserted in the center emerges clean.

5. Cut the loaf cake into slices and serve warm.

BUTTERSCOTCH CHOCOLATE CHIP BLONDIES

Here's a gooey and golden-hued mash-up of blondies and brownies. So now you can indulge in the best of both worlds.

HERE'S WHAT YOU NEED

1 pound (455 g) dark brown sugar
¾ cup (1½ sticks, or 165 g) unsalted butter, plus more for preparing the baking pan
2 tablespoons (28 ml) vanilla extract
2 large eggs
2 cups (250 g) all-purpose flour
2 teaspoons baking powder
½ teaspoon salt
1 cup (175 g) semisweet chocolate chips
1 cup (240 g) butterscotch chips

HERE'S WHAT YOU GET

30 CHEWY BLONDIES

HERE'S WHAT YOU DO

1. Melt the brown sugar and butter in a small saucepan on low heat, stirring often so that the sugar doesn't burn. Stir to combine and then set aside to cool to room temperature. Meanwhile, preheat the oven to 350°F (180°C, or gas mark 4) and generously butter a 9 x 13-inch (23 x 33 cm) baking pan.

2. When the butter mixture is cool, using a handheld electric mixer, beat in the vanilla and the eggs one at a time.

3. Sift the flour, baking powder, and salt together in a large bowl and stir to combine. Using a spatula or wooden spoon, stir the chocolate chips and butterscotch chips into the flour mixture.

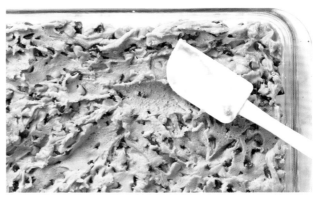

4. Pour the butter mixture into the flour mixture and stir to combine everything evenly. Spread the batter into the baking pan.

5. Bake until lightly brown and a toothpick inserted in the center comes out clean, 20 to 30 minutes. Let the blondies cool on a wire cooling rack for about 10 minutes and then cut them into 2-inch (5 cm) squares.

SNAPPY LEMON TARTLETS

Store-bought phyllo is a gift from the gods, truly. This recipe couldn't be simpler to put together, but a plate or platter of these mini filled cups will look extremely impressive and taste flat-out sweet-tart delicious. It's not that hard to make lemon curd from scratch, but there are many high-quality store-bought versions available as well.

HERE'S WHAT YOU NEED

1 lemon
1 jar of your favorite lemon curd
15 mini phyllo shells, thawed
½ cup (30 g) whipped cream

HERE'S WHAT YOU GET

15 TANGY BITE-SIZE CUPS

Variation

As an alternative, you can do the same with lime curd and squares of lime zest or orange curd and squares of orange zest. Or for a crowd, make up a big platter of all three kinds.

HERE'S WHAT YOU DO

1. Peel a few strands of lemon peel and cut into ¼-inch (6 mm) squares. You want 15 squares altogether. Try to be careful to avoid any of the white pith from the lemon peel, which will taste bitter.

3. Top each filled cup with a small dollop of whipped cream.

4. Garnish each filled cup with a lemon zest square. Serve immediately.

2. Spoon a bit of lemon curd into each phyllo cup, filling the cups to the top.

SIMPLE CHOCOLATE TRUFFLES

Store-bought truffles, though beautiful, can be hideously expensive. Here's a back-to-basics template for rolled truffles that are so rich and delicious, you'll be breaking out the recipe whenever there's the slightest occasion. There are a few variations at the end, but play around with more! The combinations are endless.

HERE'S WHAT YOU NEED

8 ounces (225 g) best-quality bittersweet chocolate, finely chopped
½ cup (120 ml) heavy cream
1 teaspoon vanilla extract
¼ cup (20 g) unsweetened cocoa powder, or more as needed

HERE'S WHAT YOU GET

ABOUT 16 - 20 HOMEMADE TRUFFLES

Variations

For mint truffles, use peppermint extract instead of vanilla. Instead of cocoa powder, roll them in finely chopped peppermint candy.

For coconut truffles, use coconut extract instead of vanilla. Instead of coconut powder, roll them in flaked coconut.

For almond truffles, use almond extract instead of vanilla. Roll in finely chopped almonds.

For orange truffles, use 1 teaspoon orange extract. Roll in superfine sugar.

HERE'S WHAT YOU DO

1. Place the chopped chocolate in a heatproof bowl. In a saucepan, heat the heavy cream to a simmer. Whatever you do, don't let it boil! Pour the hot cream over the chocolate in the bowl. Add the vanilla and let the mixture stand undisturbed for a few minutes. The heat from the cream will melt the chocolate.

3. When the mixture is cold and hard, using a small melon baller or a teaspoon, scoop out the chocolate and, with your hands, roll the chocolate into a small ball. Try to work with each ball of chocolate quickly since the heat from your hands will melt the chocolate. Place the balls on a baking sheet.

2. With a rubber spatula, stir the mixture to make sure the chocolate is fully melted and everything is well combined (the mixture should be smooth and glossy). Pour the mixture into an 8-inch (20 cm) pie plate, using the spatula to scrape every bit out of the bowl. Let cool to room temperature and then place in the refrigerator to firm up for at least 4 hours.

4. When you have finished forming the truffles, place the cocoa powder on another large plate. Roll the truffles in the cocoa powder in order to totally cover their surfaces. Return the truffles to the baking sheet and refrigerate.

5. Let the truffles stand at room temperature for 20 minutes to soften a bit before serving.

CARROT CAKE CUPCAKES

You know the crumbly kind of cupcakes that fall apart into tiny bits before you can eat them? Well, these are not like that. They are rich and creamy and hold their shape.

HERE'S WHAT YOU NEED

CUPCAKES:

3 large eggs

1½ cups (300 g) granulated sugar

1 cup (235 ml) vegetable oil

1½ teaspoons vanilla extract

3 cups (375 g) all-purpose flour

1½ teaspoons baking soda

2 teaspoons ground cinnamon

½ teaspoon ground allspice

3 cups (330 g) grated carrots (about 3 large)

1 cup (120 g) finely chopped walnuts

ICING:

4 tablespoons (55 g) unsalted butter, softened

1 package (8 ounces, or 225 g) of cream cheese, softened

2 cups (240 g) confectioners' sugar, sifted

1 teaspoon vanilla extract

HERE'S WHAT YOU GET

24 SCRUMPTIOUS CUPCAKES

HERE'S WHAT YOU DO

1. Preheat the oven to 350°F (180°C, or gas mark 4). Line two 12-muffin pans with cupcake liners. In a large bowl using a handheld electric mixer, beat the eggs and sugar together until the sugar is dissolved. Add the vegetable oil and vanilla and mix well.

2. Sift all of the dry ingredients for the cupcakes into another bowl. Use a wooden spoon to mix the dry ingredients into the egg mixture, making sure the dry ingredients are well incorporated.

3. Fold in the carrots and walnuts and then divide the batter evenly into the 24 muffin cups. Bake for 25 to 30 minutes until a toothpick inserted into the cakes come out clean. Let the cupcakes cool to room temperature.

4. To make the icing, beat the butter and cream cheese together until light and fluffy. Slowly beat in the confectioners' sugar ½ cup (60 g) at a time until well incorporated. Add the vanilla and beat to combine. Transfer the icing to a disposable plastic storage bag (or a pastry bag, if you have one) and snip ¼ inch (6 mm) off the corner of the bag. Squeeze gently to pipe the icing onto the cupcakes.

5. Refrigerate if not serving the cupcakes right away, but let them come to room temperature before serving.

QUICK ICE CREAM SANDWICHES

Store-bought ice cream sandwiches almost always have a chocolate top and bottom and vanilla ice cream inside. That can get awfully boring. How about peanut butter cookies for the outside and chocolate ice cream in the middle? Or lemon cookies with strawberry ice cream? Making your own ice cream sandwiches is easy, and the flavor combos are infinite.

HERE'S WHAT YOU NEED

⅔ pint (190 g) ice cream (flavor of your choice)
8 cookies (3 inches, or 7.5 cm in diameter; flavor of your choice)

HERE'S WHAT YOU GET

4 CHILLY SANDWICHES

A TASTY TIP To dress up your ice cream sandwiches with sprinkles, chopped nuts, or chocolate chips, place them in a shallow bowl or plate and roll the sides of the sandwich in the sprinkles, nuts, or chips to coat the ice cream before wrapping and freezing.

HERE'S WHAT YOU DO

1. Let the ice cream stand at room temperature for 4 to 6 minutes to soften up a bit. Don't let it get so soft that it will melt out the edges of your sandwiches.

2. Working quickly, scoop about ⅓ cup (47 g) of ice cream onto the bottom part of 4 of the cookies.

3. Top the ice cream with the bottom part of another cookie and press lightly to form a sandwich.

4. Wrap the ice cream sandwiches tightly in plastic wrap.

5. Place the sandwiches in the freezer and leave them there for 2 to 3 hours until they are firm.

COOL (AND HOT) THINGS to DRINK

ORANGE MINT PUNCH

This is a refreshing drink to cool things down at a hot summer barbecue. It's also easy to make this in large quantities for a party and a good excuse to pull out that punch bowl that's been languishing in the back of your cupboard.

HERE'S WHAT YOU NEED

MINT SYRUP:
2 cups (400 g) sugar
4 cups (950 ml) water
2 cups (70 g) loosely packed fresh mint leaves
PUNCH:
Orange juice
Ginger ale
Ice cubes, for serving
Mint sprigs, for garnish

HERE'S WHAT YOU GET

ENOUGH MINT-INFUSED SYRUP
FOR 8 TO 10 SERVINGS OF PUNCH

A TASTY TIP For an adult cocktail, add 1½ to 2 ounces (42 to 60 ml) vodka or rum to the glass.

HERE'S WHAT YOU DO

1. To make the syrup, in a large saucepan, mix the sugar and water and bring to a boil. Reduce the heat and simmer for 5 minutes until all the sugar dissolves.

3. Strain out the mint leaves, pour the syrup into a jar, and refrigerate until ready to use.

4. For each serving of punch, fill a tall glass with ice cubes. Add ⅓ cup (80 ml) of the syrup, ½ cup (120 ml) of orange juice, and ½ cup (120 ml) of ginger ale. Give it a quick stir, garnish with a mint sprig, and serve.

2. Place the mint leaves in a heatproof bowl. Remove the saucepan from the heat, pour the hot liquid over the mint leaves, stir, and let sit at room temperature to infuse the mint into the syrup for 2 to 3 hours.

SOUTHERN-STYLE SWEET PEACH ICED TEA

It gets hot—really hot—in the American South, and residents there are pretty expert at finding ways to keep cool in the summertime. We should all take their advice, especially when it involves drinks like this one.

HERE'S WHAT YOU NEED

PEACH SYRUP:
2 peaches, diced
1 cup (200 g) sugar
1 cup (235 ml) water
1 teaspoon vanilla extract
1 teaspoon ground cinnamon
TEA:
8 cups (2 L) water
4 black teabags
Ice cubes, for serving
Peach slices, for garnish

HERE'S WHAT YOU GET

8 TO 12 THIRST-QUENCHING SERVINGS

A TASTY TIP For an adult cocktail, add 1½ to 2 ounces (42 to 60 ml) of bourbon or gin to the glass.

HERE'S WHAT YOU DO

1. Mix the peaches, sugar, water, vanilla, and cinnamon together in a saucepan. Bring to a boil.

3. Turn the heat off and let sit at room temperature for 2 to 3 hours to infuse the peaches into the syrup. Strain out the peaches, pour the syrup into a jar, and refrigerate until ready to use.

2. Turn the heat down and simmer the mixture for 10 minutes, crushing the peaches into the liquid with a wooden spoon.

4. Make the tea by bringing the 8 cups (2 L) of water to a boil in a pot. Turn off the heat, add the teabags, and steep for 8 minutes. Remove the teabags. Let the tea cool a bit and then refrigerate until ready to serve.

5. For each drink, fill a tall glass with ice cubes. Pour in ¼ cup (60 ml) chilled peach syrup and add 1 cup (235 ml) of cold tea. Garnish with a peach slice and serve.

WATERMELON AGUA FRESCA

Agua fresca is Spanish for "cool water," and these refreshing blended drinks are found all over Mexico and the southern United States and increasingly throughout the United States. Often, some kind of melon is the main ingredient, but mango, papaya, guava, and other fruits are popular, too.

HERE'S WHAT YOU NEED

3 cups (450 g) chopped ripe watermelon
⅓ cup (80 ml) fresh lime juice (3 to 4 limes)
⅓ cup (107 g) agave nectar or (115 g) honey
Ice cubes, for serving
Soda water, for serving
Lime slices, for garnish

HERE'S WHAT YOU GET

4 TASTE-OF-SUMMER SERVINGS

A TASTY TIP For an adult cocktail, add 2 ounces (60 ml) of tequila or rum to the glass.

HERE'S WHAT YOU DO

1. Put the chopped watermelon, lime juice, and agave nectar or honey in a blender.

3. For each serving, fill a pint (475 ml) glass with ice cubes. Pour ½ cup (120 ml) of the watermelon mixture over the ice. Top it off with soda water, garnish with a lime slice, and serve right away.

2. Blend until combined and smooth. You should have about 2 cups (475 ml) of juice.

MALTED ROOT BEER FLOATS

We were once talking with a friend who had, a year prior, emigrated from Russia to the United States. In the course of the conversation, we learned that she had never tasted root beer, and this seemed astonishing. We'd like to serve her this all-American float.

HERE'S WHAT YOU NEED

1 pint (285 g) vanilla ice cream
1 quart (950 ml) root beer
4 tablespoons (55 g) crushed
   malted milk balls

HERE'S WHAT YOU GET

4 FLOATS FOR KIDS OF ALL AGES

Variation

If you want to make this a grownups-only drink, use Guinness stout instead of root beer. "Guinness is good for you," or so goes the slogan.

HERE'S WHAT YOU DO

1. About 2 hours before you want to make the floats, put 4 pint (450 ml) glasses or milk shake glasses in the freezer to chill.

3. Add the root beer. It will bubble up, so wait for the bubbles to subside and then add more root beer to fill the glass.

4. Garnish with 1 tablespoon (15 g) of the crushed malted milk balls. Serve with both a spoon and a straw.

2. Working with one glass at a time, scoop 2 scoops of ice cream (about ¼ cup, or 35 g for each scoop) into the frozen glass.

SPICED HOT CHOCOLATE

Cinnamon, cardamom, and black pepper, along with the bittersweet chocolate, make this a decidedly sophisticated hot chocolate. But don't worry—adding a puff of whipped cream or a big ol' giant marshmallow will bring it back down to earth.

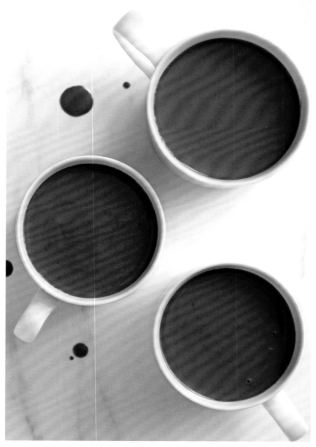

HERE'S WHAT YOU NEED

4 cups (950 ml) whole milk
½ cup (100 g) sugar
10 ounces (280 g) bittersweet chocolate, finely chopped
1 teaspoon vanilla extract
1 teaspoon ground cinnamon
1 teaspoon ground cardamom
½ teaspoon freshly cracked black pepper
¼ teaspoon salt
Marshmallows or whipped cream, for serving (optional)

HERE'S WHAT YOU GET

4 LUXURIOUS SERVINGS

A TASTY TIP For an adult hot drink, add 1 ounce (28 ml) of bourbon or rum to each mug.

HERE'S WHAT YOU DO

1. Combine the milk and sugar in a saucepan over medium-high heat. Bring to a simmer while whisking to melt the sugar, about 5 minutes. Don't let the milk boil.

3. Add the vanilla, cinnamon, cardamom, cracked pepper, and salt and stir to combine.

4. Divide the hot chocolate among 4 mugs. Garnish with marshmallows or whipped cream if you like.

2. Add the chopped chocolate and continue whisking until all the chocolate is dissolved.

MOSTLY LEMON MILK SHAKES

"Lemon" probably isn't the flavor that first comes to mind when you think "milk shake." But imagine instead a lemon cream pie, and then you'll have the "aha" moment. This cool, creamy, citrusy surprise goes down way too easy.

HERE'S WHAT YOU NEED

1 cup (140 g) vanilla ice cream
1 cup (150 g) lemon sorbet
1 cup (235 ml) whole milk
¼ cup (60 ml) orange juice

HERE'S WHAT YOU GET

2 HEDONISTIC OR 4 RESTRAINED SERVINGS

Variation

For a tarter version, use fresh lime juice instead of the orange juice.

HERE'S WHAT YOU DO

3. Divide the milk shake among glasses and serve immediately.

1. Combine the ice cream, lemon sorbet, milk, and orange juice in a blender.

2. Blend on high speed until the mixture is thick and smooth.

TRIPLE BERRY MINT SMOOTHIES

This is seriously nutritious smoothie territory, with loads of fruit, yogurt, and milk and the digestion-enhancing qualities of fresh mint. Plus, it's portable. It's a great way to start a busy day right or have an energizing snack mid-afternoon.

HERE'S WHAT YOU NEED

1 banana, sliced
1 cup (250 g) frozen raspberries
1 cup (155 g) frozen blueberries
1 cup (149 g) frozen strawberries
2 tablespoons (12 g) minced fresh mint
1 cup (230 g) plain yogurt
½ cup (120 ml) milk
8 to 10 ice cubes

HERE'S WHAT YOU GET

2 LARGE OR 4 SMALL SERVINGS

A TASTY TIP If you bring this to work for a healthy afternoon pick-me-up, store it in the office freezer rather than the fridge. You'll just have to remember to take it out a bit before you want to drink it.

HERE'S WHAT YOU DO

3. Divide the smoothie among 2 or 4 glasses and serve immediately.

1. Place the sliced banana, frozen raspberries, frozen blueberries, frozen strawberries, and minced mint in a blender and process on high speed until well blended.

2. Add the yogurt, milk, and ice cubes to the blender and process again until smooth.

CHOCOLATE STRAWBERRY SMOOTHIES

If you want to have chocolate for breakfast but don't feel that it's necessarily the best of options, try this healthful smoothie made with unsweetened cocoa powder and sweetened with honey. You will feel virtuous and like you're indulging yourself.

HERE'S WHAT YOU NEED

1 banana, sliced
3 cups (510 g) strawberries, sliced
¼ cup (20 g) unsweetened cocoa powder
¼ cup (85 g) honey
¾ cup (180 g) plain yogurt
½ cup (120 ml) milk
8 to 10 ice cubes

HERE'S WHAT YOU GET

2 LARGE BREAKFAST SERVINGS OR
4 SNACK-SIZED SERVINGS

HERE'S WHAT YOU DO

3. Divide the smoothie among 4 glasses and serve immediately.

1. Combine the sliced banana, strawberries, cocoa powder, and honey in a blender and blend on high speed until smooth.

2. Add the yogurt, milk, and ice cubes to the blender and blend again until smooth.

INDEX

7/18